MAY I SPEAK?

MAY I SPEAK?

DIARY OF A CROSSOVER TEACHER

by

Manie Culbertson

Edited and Introduction by Sue Eakin

PELICAN PUBLISHING COMPANY
GRETNA 1972

Manufactured in the United States of America
Book design by Oscar Richard
Jacket design by Gerald Bower
Published by Pelican Publishing Company, Inc.
630 Burmaster Street
Gretna, Louisiana, 70053

Dedicated to Sam and Myrtle Lyles,
*two Louisiana educators
for whom we hold the highest regard*

Contents

"MAY I SPEAK?" is a part of one of the folkways apparently developed in Louisiana's segregated Negro schools over the decades.

Startled white teachers have discovered the phrase is only a ritual, not a question, seeking permission for interruptions of classes that have seemed incredible to teachers accustomed to the routine of the white schools. One "crossover" teacher reported in amazement that a small boy appeared at the door of her first-grade class and asked: "May I speak?" He then walked to his sister's desk, took a bite of her candy and left.

"May I Speak?" seems particularly appropriate for this request for time.

MAY I SPEAK?

Introduction

This is meant to be a happy story.

It is certainly not happy in its past, but that *is the past* and nothing can change that. It is not happy in its fulfillment, for mostly that is yet to come, not only in Newton Parish* (county) and Louisiana but all over the nation. It is a happy story, then, in its promise of what can be our present and our future. It is happy too in the reassurance we Americans so deeply need that there is a steel-like strength, a capacity for doing, a delightful ingenuity in finding new answers, and a basic good will among such hardworking people as the black and white educators in high and low positions in Newton Parish who are doing their jobs without thought of glory. The immediate return, rather, is more apt to be cutting criticism from all sides, scorn from those who think there is a miraculous way somewhere to un-do more than a century of trying to go in two directions; arrogance from those on both sides who claim the other has no right to its pain and anguish in the present confused situation. But this story suggests that the answer is coming, and it is coming from the undramatic happenings of ordinary people bent on educating children who listen to both sides but are not turned from their work by either.

Manie Culbertson's diary was kept for a semester

---

* The name of the parish has been changed.

after she was transferred during the middle of the school year from a school with an all-white faculty and a student body that had experienced only token integration under court orders. Mrs. Culbertson was sent to teach in an all-Negro school, where she was among the first white teachers ("honkies") assigned to bring the faculty's white-to-black ratio to 60/40 in compliance with federal court orders. In her parish, the older and more experienced teachers were used for this step in integrating the formerly segregated schools; in some other parishes over the state, the younger and less experienced were transferred. She went feeling that it was she who had suffered discrimination, that after nearly two decades of dedicated teaching her personal preferences were totally overlooked in the carrying out of court orders. She did not wish to leave her work, both because it was her life (she loved teaching children) and because she knew that she could not find comparable compensation, including her investment in retirement, anywhere else. So, reluctantly, even fearfully, she went to the school to which she was assigned.

Indubitably, this overwhelming fear on the part of a white going into a black school will be interpreted and misinterpreted, according to a reader's individual experience or perspective. One must not probe for any deeply hidden psychological "hang-up" over white confrontation with black other than fear of physical safety. In an atmosphere charged with resentment on both sides and fanned by excited news media, a white teacher, going into this particular black school, might well anticipate trouble, as Mrs. Culbertson did. Since knifing, shooting, and fighting to settle differences were said to be part of the ghetto-like milieu of which Glenview school is a part, she was afraid. She was afraid, with or without reason, to teach in this all-black school.

This is a story unconcerned with placing blame or guilt or scorn; it is the completely honest daily record of *one white teacher* placed against her will in an all-Negro classroom. What happened in other comparable situations, even in the same school, is not known nor implied except where specific reference is made to a particular incident or person. Least of all is this one account meant to preface generalizations about the infinite complexities of white and Negro schools and the even more intricate complexities of integration of blacks and whites in a unitary system. This is meant to be one thing and one thing only: a stringently honest impression of one crossover teacher, admittedly prejudiced, afraid, and resentful about the transfer, teaching in one all-black school described. Each individual's perception of events is unique, and in this light Manie Culbertson presents her findings.

Names have been changed to assure privacy to those involved: the names of the students, faculty, school and friends of the writer are unimportant. It is the nameless teachers, administrators, and schools all over the South where such a diary might have been kept that are important, for in all the noise and confusion many do not know that these people exist at all. Like Manie Culbertson, the educators are closing their doors against all the confusion and blabbering, the noise and commotion, and simply doing a good job of teaching and learning.

One proposition that this story suggests is that it is not the courts, nor the school patrons, nor the school board members and administrators but the classroom teachers who ultimately determine the education of our children. At no time, perhaps, in Louisiana's labored history has more depended upon the quality of teachers who are implementing a new philosophy of education— public education for all students under a unitary system.

In Newton Parish, like the rest of the South and the nation, men, women, and children are going through the tortures of radical change in the emerging concept of the American Negro. If he is not so God-like as black extremists paint him, neither is he so lowly as many a white wants to portray him. The truth is somewhere in between. And to help him better himself, both black and white leaders have to accept the fact that the place to begin is with the situation as it is, not as emotional blacks and whites *imagine* it is. The Negro is simply part of the human race—sometimes brilliant, sometimes stupid, good and bad, triumphant and erring, and certainly increasingly conscious of his own racial heritage.

That the Negro began his life as a slave in a country experimenting with democracy has given him a unique background. The southern Negro has lived mostly within a subculture, protected in his own world like a moth in a cocoon. The shock whites experienced in realizing that the same rules that governed white schools had not been applied to black schools, is, at least partly, because of a recognition by administrators that black schools were going to be run in keeping with black culture. What was overlooked was the fact that students eventually had to compete in the predominant culture in which the Negro is a minority.

The Negro's subculture has been as different as Chinatown's from the dominant white culture in the United States. Within his subculture, family patterns shaped during the years of slavery; ideas of right and wrong when helplessly pitted as a slave against a master race; attitudes borne in the subservient and dependent role in the patriarchal planter-sharecropper/tenant relationship; economic patterns and social values have all been apart from the dominant culture whose theme has been equality, exclusive of the slave or his descendants. Sometimes culture and subculture have shared concepts of desirable goals, sometimes not. Now they must merge as one, the Negro managing to maintain his identity in the process as other ethnic groups have preserved theirs while uniting to work together toward fulfillment of the American dream of a good life for everybody.

Historians a century from now may find it incredible that the average southern white citizen, the Newton Parish average man or any other, went along his way until 1970 honestly believing that in recent years, at least, the Negro was provided with an equal, if segregated and separate, opportunity for education. One can hardly blame the future social scientist if he does make the error of doubting the shock the white man suffered in the discovery that this idea was totally wrong. It is hard to believe that two schools, one on one side of a railroad track, the other on the other side, so close it would scarcely take less than ten minutes to move from one to the other, could be so isolated from each other that one did not know what the other was doing, nor that the community beyond the schools involved did not know what either was doing. But this was so. The blatant truth was that an expensive school plant and equal teachers' salaries provided for black schools (often the new school plants built for Negroes before and after 1954 were far superior to the older, deteriorated buildings of the whites) did not radically change the calibre of black education, least of all secure equal opportunity for education to black students.

One fact that may elude the unwary in this connection is that social distance may well prove more formidable than mere physical distance. The social barriers existing between members of these two societies, erected over more than a century with consummate care, have seemed impregnable. It is true the Negroes shared many experiences as observers in the white community and undoubtedly knew more of white society than most whites knew about the Negro community.

In spite of the fact that the Negro school has been more modern and commodious (built in anticipation of the court order against segregation that came in 1954) and that materials have been provided on the same basis as for white schools, the Negro school in Newton Parish, in Louisiana, in the South, has operated in a different society, a different culture, with different ways of doing things that, somehow, never seemed important to either blacks or whites until now. Lest we get in a hurry to blame somebody, the biggest mistake on both sides was failure to recognize the frustrating problems of a people trapped in a subculture with towering economic and social problems from which relatively few individuals in the past have extricated themselves to merge into the dominant society and culture. The transition for the Negro, inevitably, must be difficult, sometimes painful, and slow. The changing of old habits, ingrained over the centuries, is a slow process. Yet he will never again be isolated in a subculture but will be an active participant in an integrated society. For this the schools must prepare him.

If the Negro has been trapped in a subculture, the white Louisianian has been strapped into a set of built-in prejudices in this culture—rigid in thinking that the Negro was incapable of learning, somehow more different from himself in mental outlook and genetic inheritance than even the dramatic black skin indicates. Most whites paid him little attention, felt no responsibility nor concern and, least of all, did not feel they owed him a debt.

Manie Culbertson's experience is only one of thousands of experiences of individuals in the process of integrating the schools; the situation in which she worked is only one of thousands with endless facets. She went into an all-black community resentful at being transferred from Timberlane, a few blocks from her home, where her son was a graduating senior that very semester. Just a few years back her husband had worked with a group to start a private school of the kind springing up all over the state and the rest of the South. She was by no means a do-gooder with the missionary idea of helping a deprived people and thereby earning sainthood of some kind. Instead she went on trial, planning to quit if it was as unbearable as she felt sure it would be. She had already been checking for jobs in other cities; she and her husband thought of moving away from Newton Parish entirely, perhaps to another state which had no such problem. So many white Louisianians, hostile and fearful over unknowns, light years away in their idea of the Negro world, can feel a kindred soul in the reluctant transferee to Glenview in 1970. She was going to do the minimum, she said, if she did stay at Glenview.

But the classroom door had not been closed long before Manie Culbertson was working her heart out to teach children who responded in a way that spurred her to go far beyond duty. She put away the conventional lesson plans, laid aside the textbooks, and set to work anew to create materials fitting the special needs of very special students.

There were uncounted Manie Culbertsons sharing these pioneering experiences in the new world a-coming in Louisiana education. She notes those she knew, her own circle of friends and colleagues, as representatives of untold others doing the same kind of work in the best way they knew: trying one thing, and if it didn't work, trying another. Once in the school, their goal was clear—the education of children.

What happened to this 1970 crossover teacher is a poignant story. One teacher, one classroom, one school is significant only in the key that this story gives to what is actually happening far from the eyes of television cameras or magazines and newspapers as they scream for sensation in recording the daily news. The transformation in Manie Culbertson's attitude toward the decision of the school board and the students to whom she became quickly committed is a story you will want to read yourself.

SUE EAKIN, *Assistant Professor of History*
LSU at Alexandria
Alexandria, Louisiana

January

January 2

The news came today. Right in the middle of the school year we are ordered to integrate into a "unitary" system—whatever that is—by February 1, 1970. I know that it means that whites will go to black schools and blacks will go to white schools and that the freedom-of-choice plan, which has worked so well here, is no longer considered adequate.

When we sat through the HEW court hearings in August, I thought we heard the judge hand down a plan to comply with HEW's demands. I thought—we all thought—we were settled for at least one more school year. And now *this*. Mid-term will be here January 26. Surely, if changes are to be made, they will be made then.

The school board is taking the issue to the circuit court to plead for a postponement until September, 1970.

January 5

Tonight, like the rest of the members of our chapter of Alpha Delta Kappa, an honorary teachers' sorority, I braved that hard, cold rain to attend a meeting, for our speaker was the president of the school board. He had been scheduled to speak on this date long before this situation developed, and I thought we were so lucky to be in a position to get some "inside" facts on what was happening. I didn't learn anything new. We had already heard that so far only faculty members are under order to cross over, but it was expected that orders to mix the students would come any day. I said that I didn't learn anything new. That's not so. I did learn one thing: the ratio of white faculty to black is sixty to forty. I had no idea there were so many Negro teachers in the parish.

After the speaker left, we talked of little else at the meeting. We all agreed that although we would hate to be transferred to a Negro school, we would much rather go ourselves than see the children moved in the middle of the school year.

January 7
                        The official orders came today. The school board's pleading didn't help. Every newscast, both radio and television, told about it. Well, we found out what "unitary" means. No school will be identified as black or white. The faculty of *every* school in the parish system will become integrated at a sixty-forty ratio. The school board has been ordered to file a plan for faculty mixing with the federal judge of this district. Everyone seems to feel that it is just a matter of days before the same orders for the students will come.

My phone has rung off the wall. Everyone is as stunned as I am. I guess that until today I didn't really believe that it was going to happen.

I wonder whether I will have to go—or if I would refuse to go if my name were chosen. I can't imagine myself being anywhere except at Timberlane. I have found my place here, and I don't want to be moved. I don't want our faculty shuffled around either. I'd hate for Kurt* to lose any of his teachers in the last semester of his senior year.

One thing is for sure—we will know soon. February 1 is not many days away. I hope that the board comes up with a plan this week.

January 8

Today the school principals were called to the central office for a meeting to discuss the proposed plan for the transfer of teachers.

My principal at Timberlane called a faculty meeting after school and told us that he would be glad to receive suggestions from anyone who had any ideas about how the transfer might best be accomplished. Sure, we have suggestions! But I don't know if they will be of any help to the school board in deciding what to do.

I wish I could come up with a plan that would guarantee my staying at Timberlane, but every idea that I have that saves me forces some of my best friends to go! I wish the school board wouldn't have a plan; it would be easier on all of us if they would just draw the names out of a hat. Maybe there will be enough volunteers so that nobody will have to be drafted.

I am getting myself into a stew just thinking about HEW. This is the top agency in this country on matters of education; how could those people believe that all of this turmoil in the middle of the school year is in the best

* The author's son.

interests of education? Why didn't this come up during the summer? Why did they wait until the students have finally settled down and are ready for the real learning time of the year? Any teacher with experience could "educate" HEW about how long it takes children to adjust to new teachers, new schools, and new classmates. Did HEW have any valid reasons for throwing out "freedom-of-choice"? Or does HEW realize the impact of new interpretations of *equal* education?

HEW is taking a beating from everyone. Some people are wondering what the initials really stand for— "Hate Every White," "Hell Either Way," or Health, Education, and Welfare.

January 9

Rumors are flying! Everyone wants to check with friends at other schools to get the latest word, and I am at the telephone for an hour or two each night. This can't go on.

Today the children in my classes began to press for information. They want to know if I am going to have to leave. I promised them that I would tell them as soon as I heard anything. They were satisfied. We talked about the possibility that I might leave and decided that we should make every minute of every day count. I told them that I had borrowed a motto from *Laugh-In* (a favorite TV show with them) and that from today on, "I'm going to 'sock it to you'."

I was glad this came up today. I have just completed a unit in history, and I have been debating with myself whether or not I should begin the next unit—the Civil

War. I'd like to teach it, and I can complete it if the children continue to work as they did today. If I *do* have to exchange places with a black, I imagine that this would be a ticklish unit to study during the adjustment period.

January 13

The school board met in secret session today to adopt a plan for faculty integration. Someone called about 6:00 p.m. to say that the details of the plan had been given on a local radio station. Now we have something else to figure out. The plan is based on seniority. I listened to every broadcast the rest of the evening, but I didn't hear any details. Seniority could be good, or it could be bad. Last year, fourth-year teachers had to cross over; so if they go on up the scale to fifth, sixth, etc., I should be in good shape. I have eighteen years of teaching experience, and surely enough teachers to meet the quota will be found before they get that high. I wish I knew something about the average teaching experience of teachers in this parish. Suddenly this has become a very interesting subject!

It's 11:00 p.m. After all the hashing and rehashing via telephone, Randy, with her twenty years of experience, and I have concluded that we are safe. Here's hoping we're right!

January 14

How low can you get? Words couldn't begin to describe my feelings tonight. I have to go.

This afternoon the principal told us how the board will choose the transferees. It will not be on a parish-wide basis after all. Each school will be considered by departments, and forty percent of each group will go. Teachers not under tenure (less than fourth year) will not be considered for transfer. Selections will be based on *present* continuous service in Newton Parish.

That did it. My years in Texas do not count, and I am low man on the totem pole in my department. Of the eight teachers in our group, five are not eligible for transfer because they don't have tenure. Jodie has seniority in the department so that leaves two of us. Claire and I are the lucky ones who get to go.

I am in a daze. I have been hardly civil to Jim* and Kurt. They are so concerned and have tried to boost my spirits, but I am feeling too sorry for myself to communicate very well. This can't be happening to me!

Later . . . Did I say that I didn't feel like communicating? I have never communicated so completely or at such length as I have done this evening.

Joe, our next-door neighbor and a biology teacher at Timberlane, with eighteen years of experience, and I got restless. I got Jim and Joe got his wife to go with us to talk to our school-board-member friend about the situation.

We felt that certain aspects of the transfer plan were not fair, and we were reasonably sure that these had not been called to the attention of the board members. For instance, for the past two years Newton has been requiring that fourth-year teachers be assigned to Negro schools. Several teachers resigned rather than accept the transfer.

* The author's husband.

They stayed out a year and then returned to the system. Now they are considered first-year teachers and are not subject to transfer.

At Timberlane the high-school English department is being stripped of almost every experienced teacher. Only one experienced junior-high "block" (a two-hour English-American history class) teacher remains. Most of our teachers who are to transfer have more than ten years of service; one has as many as twenty-nine years.

We wondered whether the board had considered the fact that third-year teachers have probably already had experience in desegregated schools, for when they did their practice teaching, the schools were mixed under the token integration plan. Many of them have already adjusted to an integrated world; they would not have to fight the prejudice that hangs on in an older generation.

We must have stayed three or four hours, and we talked constantly for the entire time. Poor man—he must be exhausted. Before we arrived, he had spent several hours on the phone talking to disgruntled teachers and parents. This is no time to be a school board member. We left with the satisfaction that we had one member of the administration who had listened to our side and was sincerely concerned about our plight.

I think I may be able to sleep tonight now. I wasn't sure earlier.

January 15

I should be like Joe, but I just can't. He's already started packing. Down deep, I feel that something is going to save me yet!

I am disgusted with myself for letting this thing bug

me so much. I wish I could get some rest from it. All day at school I hear it. People don't say "hello" anymore; they greet you with, "How long have you been in the parish? Do you have to transfer?" Then, when I get home, if someone doesn't phone me, I pick up the phone to check on some friend in another school. There is no way to get away from it all. You can't watch TV, read the paper, or even go to church without facing this horrible problem.

Some parents and teachers call to sympathize. A friend just called to say, "I'm sorry; I just wanted you to know that I'm thinking about you." Her crying drowned out the rest of her remarks.

Another friend called, but she quickly changed the subject when her husband got within hearing range. She had already told me that he had been very emphatic: "Quit. If you go, it will be against my wishes. If you decide to go, I don't want to hear one word about it." And she said he meant that he didn't want her to discuss it in any form or fashion.

I don't know what I'd do if I had that problem added to this impossible one. Jim and Kurt are good psychiatrists—they just listen to me and all my friends.

When I try to get settled, my mind is racing with the unanswered questions that haunt me. Sleep—what I wouldn't give for some sleep!

January 18

What a miserable Sunday this was!
Another Timberlane teacher, who expects to be moved, and I went out this afternoon in a pouring rain

to try to locate the Negro schools in this area to which we will probably be sent. We had some misgivings as we drove into the Johnson Road community, one of the largest all-Negro settlements in the country with an estimated population of 17,000. This area has been "off-limits" to white women for years, but we knew no other way to reach Glenview High School, our probable assignment. White teachers in our school feel that this is the worst assignment one could get, and the way our luck is running, we feel sure we'll get it. We wandered around until we found Pop Corn Street. This we couldn't resist following. It took us to Glenview. I can't really describe it; my eyes filled with tears when I saw that the colors used on the trim on the school were the blue and white of my beloved Timberlane.

We made our way back to the highway and set out for Clinton, the only other junior-senior Negro school in the northern part of the parish. We must have driven fifteen miles, only to get to the middle of nowhere. That has to be the loneliest spot in the state. Beer cans and trash littered the grounds.

We started home by another route, hoping to find more signs of civilization along the way, but it was just as lonely. I'd be terrified if I had car trouble along that road.

We passed through the town where our school-board-member friend lives and decided to stop to talk with him again. He couldn't believe our reports about the grounds at Clinton. He told us that it was considered to be one of the cleanest schools in the country.

Maybe it was the rainy day. I hope so. I am bluer than blue tonight.

January 19

It's official. The list of transferees came today. Rumor had warned us that this was the day, but I wasn't really prepared.

When I received a call from the school secretary telling me that the principal wanted to see me before I left school, I knew that was it. My memory of my visit to his office is like a bad dream. I was numb as I heard him say, "You'll never know how sorry I am to do this. Take this slip and hand it in tomorrow."

I left his office with that paper in my hand, feeling that the world had come to an end. I passed a long line of teachers, still waiting to get into the office to be told the same thing. Some of them were crying.

I hadn't read the slip the principal handed me. I went into the teachers' lounge to read it. It was very simple and to the point. It asked that I choose three Negro schools in the order of my preference. I hadn't even considered any schools other than Glenview and Clinton, but during the next hour I heard the pros and cons of every Negro school in the parish.

I still don't know what to put on that paper. It asks for three choices, but I don't want to go anywhere. I don't want to leave Timberlane. He didn't say what to do in that case. But I think I know—either I make my choice or someone else will do it for me.

My neighbor, Joe, came in to tell me that he didn't have to leave. A teacher of physical science was chosen from his department. If I had stayed in home economics, I wouldn't be leaving either. There are so many teachers eligible for transfer in that department that my seniority would have saved me.

We do not know when the transfer will take place.

We haven't heard anything more about the student transfers either.

When the principal asked for our suggestions earlier, we might have tried to work out a plan if we had known that this was the method being considered. Our neighboring parish has already made its change; the least experienced teachers moved. Newton teachers are upset about this—their plan seems so much fairer than our plan.

I'm not sure about my own feelings. I'm frustrated! I'm too much a part of the whole problem to think clearly, but I do know one thing for sure. I have been embarrassed for my own profession when I have heard cutting remarks made to beginning teachers. They didn't make the rules, and they know that they will automatically transfer the fourth year, so why punish them?

The consensus is that the board feared that inexperienced teachers would be unable to handle the discipline problems that are likely to follow the student transfers. Some have proposed that the board feared that the younger teachers would resign to look for other work, but I don't think so. The younger ones expected to be sent, and they aren't nearly as disturbed as the older folks about integration, since they became accustomed to it in college. It's true; they have less to lose if they do quit.

The more experienced teachers are not financially independent enough to quit. They would sacrifice higher-paying jobs for lower-paying ones elsewhere, probably. They would have to give up many of their accrued retirement benefits and insurance and, oh, yes, seniority. Seniority used to mean security. It's a mixed-up world where experience is rewarded with the most unpleasant assignment.

January 20

I never knew before what insomnia is, but I found out last night. What an experience! A nightmare without sleep. Then today the aftermath of loss of sleep. I was nauseated all day. I couldn't concentrate on teaching. I told the children that my name was on the list. Most of them took it very well.

My nausea bothered me during the morning, and I kept going back and forth to the lounge to get Cokes. The assistant principal noticed how queasy I was and asked if I would like to take my class to hear a talk about the police department. She will never know how glad I was to take them. I don't know what the talk was about. All I wanted was to have a few minutes when I didn't have to think.

Eventually the time came when those slips had to be turned in. After listening to all that scuttlebutt in the lounge yesterday about the advantages and disadvantages of going to this or that school, I decided to fill in just one blank. I wrote that I wanted to go wherever the Timberlane seventh graders were sent. Somehow I feel that if my class and I are sent to the same place, we will make it. I know that my students feel that way, too. We are expecting student transfer plans to be announced any day. They are growing as uneasy as the teachers are.

January 21

The students got rid of some of their pent-up feelings today. From 3,000 to 5,000 students from the entire parish marched on the federal building today to protest busing and the breaking-up of their schools in the middle of the year. The students marched about five miles, from the auction barn to downtown Vandalia. According to the news tonight, the march was very orderly. Many carried banners protesting the transfer of their teachers—their "best" teachers, too, so they said!

Their protest was well-timed but ineffective, for the board presented a geographic zoning plan for school attendance to the judge today. The most drastic changes will be at the senior-high level, where several formerly Negro high schools will be closed, and the students will be transferred to formerly white schools. If the judge approves the plan, the transfers will be made by stages. The elementary children will move first, followed by the junior high, and finally the senior high.

Timberlane will not see much change this year, as our school district cannot be changed until the new high school on the Johnson Road is completed. Opening date for that school, now designated only as Project 131, is January, 1971. We will get some new students, but not many Timberlane students will leave.

My seventh-graders do not have to move. Wouldn't it be wonderful if the board honored my preference slip? No such luck. I guess this leaves me subject to assignment anywhere they want to send me. How happy I am for my students! They will have heard this on the news, as I did. I can hardly wait to see their faces in the morning.

I think we are all relieved that the geographic plan was submitted. There has been much talk that HEW favored a pairing system, which would have paired Timberlane with Glenview, one being the junior high and the other the senior high.

This worry is taking its toll with me. I dread going to bed to toss and turn for hours. Sleep would get me out of my misery for a while.

I keep thinking about all the things that might happen to me in an all-black school. I'm a peace lover at heart, and the thought of physical violence scares me to death. I keep recalling every horrible story that I've heard for years about the violence that characterizes the Negro community. Think: "There's nothing to fear but fear itself." Maybe the author of that consoling thought has the right idea. I'll go to sleep on that one.

January 22

I was prepared for happy, smiling faces this morning, but that is not what I found when my class entered. They were so upset that it was difficult to have class. They told me that a walkout was brewing. They knew that the high-school students were making plans, and they were angry that they were not being allowed to take part in the excitement.

The children were right. Printed notices confirming the plan for a walkout tomorrow were in almost all of the students' and teachers' hands by the end of the day.

What a horrible time to live through!

FREEDOM OF CHOICE RALLY

PROTESTING SCHOOL CHANGE IN THE MIDDLE
OF THE YEAR

*Everyone should have the right to attend
the school of his choice.*

WHERE: Timberlane High School
WHEN: January 23, 1970, 9:00 a.m., Friday
         Meet outside on the ramp for a sit-in

January 23

I felt sorry for the students today. Their walkout was a fizzle. They chose a time without considering that it fell right in the middle of a class period. Very few had the nerve to get up and walk out while a lesson was going on. If they had set the time to fall between classes, I think it would have been a total success. Poor kids! They just don't like what's going on, and isn't this the way we all feel?

I heard tonight that protests of this kind were staged in many schools. The Negro students are especially enraged at the thought of losing their high schools. Rumor again—we hear that at one Negro high school the students are boasting that no white will cross the doorstep.

We are probably in for a rough time before this year is over.

January 26

The final blow to us transferees came today. We were handed a list of things that we must do before we leave. We don't yet know where we are going or when we are to leave. I suppose they want us to be ready at a minute's notice. I am so exhausted from worry that when I looked at that list, I felt that I faced an impossible task. This is one time that I won't get the job done. All my spirit is gone.

January 27

Tonight about 200 teachers responded to a call meeting at the Community Center to discuss the school board's proposal. I went with a group from Timberlane. Not all of the ones in our carpool are transferees. Some went to see if they could help us. An interesting conversation on the way to town included these remarks:

"Being labeled 'best' has been the reward for our years of service," one transferee remarked. "I've never had so many compliments before in my twenty-five years of teaching! 'Our best teachers are leaving' sounds good anyway."

Another teacher quickly said, "I wish the public would quit saying 'best' and say 'experienced'."

I listened to the conversation, but I kept my thoughts to myself. Is this the public's way of sympathizing? People are aware that experienced teachers aren't always the best, but they also realize that the kind words ease our feelings some. The transferees surely cannot complain about the response from the general public. We've had our share of praise and sympathy.

I am not sure that anything was accomplished at the meeting except that the board has undeniable evidence that many, many teachers are unhappy. Surely some modifications will be made before the plan is put into effect.

January 28

I called the parish superintendent when I got in from school today. He was not in his office, but the secretary took my number. I felt that I had to make some effort to make him see how teachers feel about the injustice that is being done to so many experienced teachers.

I can't go! I am not ready to move over and live in such a different world. Just when I think I am getting hold of myself, something comes along and knocks the props from under me. Today we received the Newton Public Schools Report, a bulletin issued by the central office to acquaint teachers and the public with facts about the school system. Negroes, Negroes, Negroes. All about Negroes, Negro teachers, Negro projects. Many Negro teachers holding choice positions are there only because they are the best qualified of their lot—not because they are so good.

About six o'clock the superintendent returned my call. He was most gracious and gave me all of the time I wanted to state my complaints. I'm sure that they were not the first he had heard today! I explained to him that I have many more years of service than some block teachers who are not on the list. It seems to me that it would be much fairer to consider service on a parish-wide basis instead of by the individual school. He said that this had been considered but had presented too many complications. The HEW requirement is for *individual* schools to be staffed sixty-forty. If the 60/40 requirement were on a parish basis, the plan could have been different.

I also pointed out that some experienced teachers were exempt from transfer because they had left this school system and returned just in time to receive preferential treatment. He had not been aware of this and promised to look into the situation. This wouldn't save me, but it would correct one evil that has caused so much bitterness. I'll have to count on something else to save me. HELP! . . . HELP! . . . HELP!!

January 30

This came today from the parish school superintendent, but it didn't satisfy the multitude of teachers who feel that the Newton Parish plan is unfair.

Some concern has been expressed relative to the procedures used in the development of criteria for transfer of teachers as required by federal court order. Such a transfer was certain to cause confusion and disappointment to many teachers.

The superintendent's office developed the plan that was ultimately adopted by the Newton Parish School Board. Realizing that the teachers with greatest experience and maturity were needed for this effort, the staff felt that continuance of the previously adopted practice of transferring teachers in compliance of court order after tenure was in the best interest of the Newton Parish School System. After the criteria for transfer were developed, the material was submitted to all of the principals and supervisors, and representatives of the executive committees of the teacher organizations.

The staff made minor adjustments in the criteria prior to the submission of the plan to the Newton Parish School Board. The school board made additional corrections prior to adoption for submission to the court. While we are appreciative of the help in finalizing the plan, the office of the superintendent must assume full responsibility for the final plan.

Newton Parish schools must continue to offer quality education to all pupils. While these are uncertain days, teachers, to a greater degree than any other segment of the community, know that federal court orders must be implemented.

We are most appreciative of the cooperative spirit of

the many teachers that have been affected by the untimely order of the federal courts.

School must go on even if the teachers are unhappy. Who asked the teachers about their feelings? It's for sure the Supreme Court or HEW didn't poll this school system.

February

We still haven't heard where **or** when. My poor principal. Usually so enthusiastic about everything, and now. . . . The teachers who are leaving feel they can't accomplish anything more with their Timberlane classes, and the teachers who are staying are so disturbed they aren't interested in holding assigned departmental meetings or doing anything else except going through the mechanics of the school day. I've never known teacher morale to be lower.

Thank goodness, I decided to introduce the Civil War unit. The students are so interested in it that we do keep busy. I know that the school day is much easier for me than it is for many.

I hope I get some sleep tonight. Last night I dreamed about this mess during the little time I did sleep. There doesn't seem to be any escape.

The elementary teachers received their new assignments today. Poor things. Many of them did not get the same subjects to teach nor the same grade level they had been teaching. It is not enough to have to change schools in the middle of the year; a teacher must change subjects and grade levels, too. That is just too much. They are a bitter group.

I checked with the teachers at Kirby, the elementary school where I worked before coming to Timberlane. I think the case of Mrs. Peck there is the saddest and cruelest in the parish. She has to be one of the finest teachers this parish has ever had. She has taught in the parish for forty years—she has Hodgkin's Disease, but she gives of herself far beyond the requirement of the job. Due to the fact that she started teaching at an early age, she could have retired several years ago and even planned to do so. Her love of teaching and her genuine concern for the welfare of children compelled her to destroy the retirement papers, which she had signed, and continue in the profession. She was assigned to a Negro school. She picked up the telephone and called the school-board office to say that she could not accept the assignment. She was told, "Then you may sign your retirement papers tomorrow." That was all. Her forty years of service meant nothing; a rule was a rule and forty percent had to go from that department.

The resignations must be staggering. My friend Janice is debating the situation. Mrs. Peck didn't have much choice.

We did learn a little more today about how things are going to be done. The mixing will be done in three steps—really more than that, for the students will not go at the same time as the teachers. The teachers will change one day, and the students at that level will not attend school that day. The white teachers will spend half a day at the black school, and then the black teachers will spend half a day in the white school. I don't know which group goes first. This came as a pleasant surprise to us. We had anticipated a "fruit-basket-turnover" situation, with everybody at one level moving at one time, which would have been catastrophic!

I am so thankful that I will not have to meet my replacement before a classroom filled with emotionally charged youngsters. I have dreaded that one moment almost more than any other part of the transfer.

This nightmare is actually taking place!

February 4

Tonight I had time to check on some of my elementary-teacher friends who had been reassigned. Several had considered resigning. Sue was assigned to Lincoln, an elementary school located in an all-Negro section of the city. She and her husband drove out to look it over. They found the school open and went in and talked with the principal. They were so favorably impressed that she decided not to resign. She says she will give it a try.

As nearly as I can figure out, assignments are being made on a geographical basis. Teachers are being sent to the schools nearest their homes or closest to their former schools. People both north and south of me have been sent to the Johnson Road area, so I guess that means Glenview for me. Clinton is the only school where Liberty teachers could be sent, so there probably won't be room for Timberlane teachers there.

February 5

Today I had a new experience. In the classroom, I have tried to speak very carefully about the Negro schools and the problems they presented, for I have several Negro students in my classes. Despite the care with which I chose my words, I had somehow offended one of my Negro students. He couldn't understand why I would be reluctant to go, nor could he accept the fact that the white students didn't want to see me go.

During class today I could tell that he was bent on no ordinary project as he wrote furiously on the paper in front of him. His eyes burned like live charcoal, and he was definitely tense—to the point of near-explosion. Since he was supposed to be participating in a class discussion, not writing, I picked up his paper. The first thing I saw was I DO NOT LIKE MRS. CULBERSON. On the back he had written his thoughts down, not too clearly so far as spelling and grammar are concerned, but the message was certainly there:

> I think that Louisiane need to iniagate because they need to love oneavery not to hirt avery state inigate. how come Louisiane do not the posent do not want white childon to go to neagro school. they think Nergro teacher cannot teach there children because negro do not enoug Education and the old people do not wanted the white children to go with the Negro children. I went to Lo Sping I saw white children playing with me.

February 6

Jim Peck, a senior at Timberlane, handed in a poem to his English teacher today. No doubt he is upset about his mother's retirement. It did us all good to read this seventeen-year-old's expression of his thoughts on this situation. I think all of us feel the same way.

A PSALM OF SCHOOL
(adapted from Longfellow's
A PSALM OF LIFE)

Tell me not in mournful numbers,
A unitary system's but a dream!
For the mind is blind that slumbers
And things are not what they seem.

School is real! School is earnest!
And education's not its goal;
But black and white will all returnest,
To brotherhood of soul to soul.

Not enjoyment, but much sorrow
Is our destined end or way;
Quality education's our gift tomorrow,
For H. E. W.'s had its say.

Learning's long, and freedom's fleeting;
And the South, though stout and brave,
Must suffer from the North's vengeful beating,
Like muffled drums from Yankee graves.

In the school's broad field of battle,
In this trying time of life,
Be not like dumb, driven cattle!
Be a hero in the strife!

Trust no leader, however pleasant;
Let the socialists bury their dead!
Overcome the oppression of the present,
And fight for liberty instead.

Judges in Washington must despise us;
They must think that we are fools;
They send court orders down upon us,
Then send their young to private schools.

The fools, they think that just by mixing,
To black and white will love impart,
But by their blind, illegal "fixing,"
The races are further torn apart.

Let us, then, be up and doing,
With a heart for any fate;
H. E. W.'s a caldron brewing,
And from it bubbles naught but hate.

February 8

Another Sunday afternoon wasted. Today I wrote a long letter to the Newton Parish School Board—which I'll never mail—to get rid of some pent-up feelings. Here we are—confronted with the most serious crisis that teachers could face—and they are stewing over where to build a new administrative office. The public is to be allowed to share in the plan, but the public was not asked to take any part in the transfer plans for teachers. Which is more important?

Psychologists are right. Writing helps release tensions, and I have plenty to release.

February 9

This was elementary teacher transfer day. The elementary children did not attend school. I talked to a few of my friends tonight. So far, so good. At Greenwall Elementary they were welcomed with a big luncheon, but most of them had already eaten. The blacks went to the white schools during the morning, and the whites crossed over during the afternoon.

The only time that I get my mind off this is during

the time I'm teaching. My "sock it to you" slogan keeps all of us going. I've explained that I want to make every minute count, so we are cramming as much as possible into these last days.

February 10

I am nauseated again. I'm in for another sleepless night. The reports from elementary teachers tonight have torn me to pieces. They say everything is horrible. I got to the point tonight that I didn't want to talk to anyone else. My head is splitting. How will I face tomorrow?

February 11

The minute I got to the school grounds today, I knew the bad news had come. The word made the rounds in the lounge that we would get our assignments today.

Just before eleven o'clock the intercom buzzed. I tried to hide my feelings from the children, but I know I must have jumped. I heard the secretary say, "The principal wants to see you immediately." I asked a student to take over the class until I could get back. It didn't take long.

He handed me a pink slip. On it was printed my assignment: Language-Arts & Social Studies, Glenview Seventh Grade. My first question was regarding the assignments of other teachers. I wondered who else was going to Glenview. He said that he'd rather not say anything until everyone had his assignment.

I stumbled into the lounge for a minute to compose

myself before facing the children. It was time for my class to go to lunch, but I could see my room from the lounge and knew that not a pupil had left his seat. I walked into the room and said, "I am going to Glenview." They just sat there. No one said a word. To them, too, Glenview was a most undesirable assignment. I was near the breaking point, and I saw tears beginning to well up in a few eyes, so I rushed them off to lunch and ran to the lounge.

In the lounge I tried with fair success to keep the tears back. I was somewhat comforted to hear that most of my co-workers were also going to Glenview. My friends were trying to be cheerful and sympathetic at the same time, and every new person who spoke to me broke my resistance down a little more with his kindness. A substitute teacher who had had my son in class the last hour said, "I told Kurt about your assignment. I didn't think you would mind. He just said, 'Oh, that's what she was expecting'."

That did it. I had one good cry, and somehow the tears relieved my tension. At least the waiting was over.

My "orders" are to report to Glenview on February 17. Two-and-a-half days left at Timberlane! I have to leave, even if I don't take my transfer. Someone else is going to take over Room 208. I can't stand the thought!

I have very little time to complete the unit of work we are doing in history. I worked so hard with my last "block" class, trying to complete our unit, that I didn't have time to feel sorry for myself until the final bell rang.

I'm so tired tonight that I'm not thinking clearly. I don't remember calling Jim to tell him that I was going to stay to start packing, but he showed up with food and stayed to help me until we finished around eight o'clock.

There were almost incessant interruptions by students, teachers, and custodial staff members saying, "I'm sorry." But that isn't the only reason it took forever to finish packing; I am not going to take my materials over to Glenview, and I wanted them packed carefully for storage. I didn't collect them for Glenview, and I have no intention of using them at Glenview. Maybe someday I will get back "home" and use them again.

After I got home, I had phone calls. My friend Randy says I am lucky to get Glenview. She has worked for the past ten years with the assistant principal who is transferring to Glenview, and she thinks she's great. I am glad to hear something *good* about Glenview. And, too, I did get the same grade and the same subjects; some weren't that lucky.

Surely I'll sleep tonight. I'm physically and mentally exhausted.

February 12

People stopped by my room all day to see whether there was something that they could do to help. I felt like saying, "Yes, call the school board to stop my transfer." Some of the boys volunteered to stay after school to help me load my boxes of materials on the truck. This I really appreciated. Jim backed the truck as close to my room as he could get, but there were still many steps to be taken. The Key Club boys came by to move a large cabinet of mine to Marian's room. It was eight o'clock again before I got home. This time all of my possessions from Timberlane were removed from Room 208. I am beginning to feel separated from Timberlane already.

I was in the house only a few minutes when an elementary school transferee called to tell me about her class. "I have wandered into a foreign land, and I feel like a missionary. In my fourth grade I have students thirteen years old. I have one 'hoodlum', Charlie. I was told that I'd better watch Charlie."

Her informer had told her, "Charlie will steal the sugar out of the cake. But there's one thing you can thank God for about Charlie!"

"What's that?"

"Charlie don't come ever' day!"

February 13

What a day!

During first period I had two corsages delivered to my room. Both were in the Valentine motif and were just beautiful. I couldn't choose between them; I wouldn't choose between them; so I wore both. A little later I received a bouquet of flowers, which I placed on my desk.

My spirits stayed pretty high today. I suppose that after I got everything moved out last night and finally realized that I was actually leaving Timberlane, it made things a little easier.

During my first "block" I was calling out spelling when the children, in unison, said, "Wait." They came up and presented me with a box of my favorite candy. Then they were ready to settle down, and they worked like angels the rest of the period. Usually seventh graders are experts at time-killing, but today they seemed to sense that this was an unusual situation and rose to the occasion.

The second "block" presented me with two long-stemmed carnations—one red and one white—and a cup tree. Then they, too, worked diligently in spite of the situation.

At three o'clock there was a faculty farewell party for the transferees. As I walked to the home-ec department, I felt as if I were on the way to my own funeral, but the party turned out to be fun. Maybe I was beginning to realize that the world was changing, but not ending. Each of us received a Timberlane charm. Someone read a funny poem. Everyone tried hard to be gay and keep things on a light basis. This worked until the time for "goodbyes" came. For me that time was almost unbearably sad, but I stayed until the end. Some were not able to do that; they sneaked away without saying anything.

When I left the building and was walking away from Timberlane, the school I had helped to start two-and-a-half years before, I had an awful sinking feeling. "Friday, the thirteenth," I thought. "My funeral day. Only this time the corpse walks out, carrying her own flowers."

Later I heard from a friend at another school that they had had a farewell cake that was "sixty-forty": sixty percent white and forty percent chocolate icing. I couldn't have taken that kind of joking today.

When I got home, Mom and Dad were waiting for me. They had driven the two-hundred miles to see how I was taking it. They tried their best to cheer me. They had brought shelled pecans and fresh fish they had caught. I was touched.

They wanted to go right away, almost before they said hello, to see the school where I would be teaching. Jim drove us to Glenview. I hadn't really seen it the other time I went there, but today I was determined to get a better picture of it in my mind. After all, this was "my" school now. The bumpy road wasn't a very good introduction, but the single-story buff-brick building and grounds were clean. Like most of the schools in Newton Parish, Glenview has its share of temporary metal buildings. It will be just my luck to be assigned to one.

The building was locked, but I could see through the window and the doors well enough to figure out the plan of the building. A long corridor with lockers on either side runs the full length of the wing. Classrooms are on both sides of the hall and have outside casement windows. This spells trouble! Maybe the temporary buildings won't be so bad. Kirby had outside windows, and I know what it is to compete with ball games, cars—any outside distraction—for the children's attention. I guess I've been spoiled by my second-floor room with stationary windows at Timberlane.

Mom and Dad had talked constantly since they arrived, but on the way home they were strangely quiet. Dad did comment that in their home district the teachers with experience were not transferred.

Tonight we sat around and talked "family" for hours. What a relief to get the transfer completely off my mind for a few hours.

February 14

Mom and Dad were ready to go when I got up this morning. They usually stay until Sunday, but they felt that I had too much to do. They were right, of course. The school board decided that we should close the grading period when we transferred, even though that made only four weeks in this grading period. This meant that I had to average grades and prepare grades for the computer. I dislike this task intensely, and it was especially annoying today.

It took my whole day to get the grades finished. I stopped once to answer the doorbell; a student came by to bring me a house plant in a beautiful container. I stopped a second time to visit by telephone with a young teacher who has been teaching in a Negro school all year. She had heard of my transfer and wanted to pass on some helpful hints.

She told me to expect to see the word "honkies" written on the blackboard, on papers—anywhere there was space to write. She said that this is the Negro equivalent of "nigger". They mean this as a derogatory word for white people. She suggested that I ignore it. HEW: Honkies Everywhere. I'm wondering whether this thought has ever occurred to them.

"They don't think about forbidden sharing of information as cheating," the "veteran" told me. "They look on work as a community problem, and it is practically impossible to get a homework assignment—or even a test paper—that is the work of the individual alone."

She sounded so discouraged about her teaching that I wanted to cry. I saw her go off to teach in a Negro school last September with stars in her eyes. She thought she could do so much good and was thrilled by the challenge it presented. She hadn't anticipated any problems. Now she is ready to leave teaching. She's not sure that forced integration is the solution for the Negro's problems.

February 15

Tomorrow I go to Glenview. This thought stayed on my mind all day. I finally decided that I would not have the energy to make the trip if I didn't relax and get some rest. I stayed in bed yesterday grading papers, but that wasn't rest. Today I put all of my work aside and went to bed in the middle of the day! I telephoned my elementary "crossover" friends, but I heard so many depressing stories of their experiences that I realize that I was defeating my purpose. I decided to call Norma, for she always sees the funny side of things. Her warm-hearted laughter is contagious. I couldn't believe my ears when I heard her saying, "If it weren't for the weekends, I couldn't make it. This week has been more than I can stand. I'm not sure that I will go back tomorrow."

I can't stand to think of tomorrow. I could quit, but I've never been a quitter and I like to teach. I could go to work somewhere else for less pay, which would certainly satisfy an enraged neighbor who told me only a day or so ago that all white teachers should refuse to go. "They're crazy for going," he told me. "Oh, they might eat turnip greens and cornbread instead of steak, but they're letting the people down by giving in to HEW."

Am I crazy for going?

February 16

I have been to Glenview, I've turned my class over to my replacement, and I have survived! Glory be!

The plan for the junior-high crossover was for the morning to be spent at the Negro school and the afternoon at the white school. I rode over to Glenview in a carpool with three other transferees from Timberlane. We were all scared stiff of what lay ahead of us. The tensions were relieved a little when Mary reminded us that the "best" teachers were transferring.

We were directed to the school auditorium when we arrived. The principal, Mr. Hudson, welcomed us and then invited the president of the student council to speak. "Get with it and be good Tigers," said the president. I hadn't counted on that. I'd rather be a Timberlane Mustang.

While the speeches went on, I sat there thinking about all the promises that I had made myself. I won't do one extra thing. I'm not going to spend hours on bulletin boards. No extras. I'll serve my sentence and deposit my paycheck. I wonder how many others in the same predicament feel just as I do.

The principal was giving some advice; I decided I'd better listen. "I know you're going to have problems, and one problem will be what to call us. I'm from the old school, and I haven't accepted this term 'blacks'. I know that my own people developed that term, but I don't like it. Some prefer to be called 'Negroes', and some prefer 'colored', but don't call them 'niggers'. The best thing to do is to avoid saying any of these. Just call them 'students'."

Somebody punched me and whispered, 'What does he think we say, 'Whites, get out your paper'?"

Mr. Hudson didn't mention anything about how to pronounce *Negro*. I know, anyway, because one of the

Negro crossovers to a white school last year instructed her faculty on the correct pronunciation by using the words *knee grow*.

Mr. Hudson gave us some more advice before he dismissed us. "Don't be afraid of these students. They're just students like any others." That made sense to me.

After the general meeting we met the teachers whom we were replacing. My predecessor, Mrs. Jones, had been transferred within the school and will be teaching math. I didn't understand that, but she didn't offer an explanation. She told me what she had covered in both English and history, and I realized that they were far behind the class I had left at Timberlane. She couldn't show me my room, because there was some question about which room I would occupy. No one mentioned the temporary buildings, however.

Refreshments were served in the cafeteria, but I couldn't eat. My stomach was in knots, and I knew that I would be sick. I wasn't too sure that I wanted to eat there. All I could think about was that Mr. Hudson had said we were free to leave after the refreshments.

We went straight back to Timberlane, where we met the Timberlane teachers who had been transferred to other schools. It was hard to believe the Wilson transferee, who told us that her assignment seemed to be all right. The Timberlane teachers who had not transferred crowded into the lounge to hear our reactions to the morning's experience.

I met with my replacement, a friendly woman with five years of teaching experience. I explained what we had done this year and what was left to do. She seemed willing to work, and I was thankful for the children's sake.

It wasn't as bad as I thought it was going to be. Now I wonder what I worried about so much. (Down deep I thought someone would stick a knife in my back or that something else horrible would happen.) It was a surprising day. I'll still take my tear-gas gun in my purse tomorrow.

Newton Parish has had at least two Negro teachers in each white school since 1967, and some white teachers have been over in the Negro schools. I had not heard how last year's token faculty integration had worked until today. I know that we can learn to work together professionally, but I hope that we won't be expected to fraternize or become involved socially the way some did in the beginning. Today's transferees came back with a story about a white teacher who had made a spectacle of himself by fawning over the Negro teachers.

The principal at Glenview had everything very well organized. He had a large envelope full of information for each of us. He certainly started things off well. There's one point I need to clarify. He gave the school hours as 7:50 to 3:30. I don't want to be out in that area thirty minutes after school is out.

It won't be as hard to go tomorrow as it was today.

February 17

Today I met my all-Negro class in my all-Negro school. I had to stop by the office to find out which room I had been assigned. The children were already there when I entered the room. They were friendly. I introduced myself briefly and then asked them to tell me what they had been studying. I checked them on parts of speech and was amazed to see how well they did. I next had them write introductions of themselves.

They seemed eager to learn and not at all displeased to have a new white teacher. Some of the elementary teachers found hostile classes, but this was not true of my classes. They were really well-behaved today.

But the noise! The noise around the school is unbelievable. I have never heard anything like it before. There is so much noise and milling around in the halls that one would think that recess goes on all day. It would be impossible to teach with the door open. At Timberlane we didn't even have doors to our rooms, yet it was relatively quiet.

My day included a two-hour class of thirty-one students, a one-hour free period, lunch, a one-hour class of twenty-one, and a two-hour class of twenty-five. Even so, I was so fired with nervous energy that I talked with friends for hours after I returned home. I called Mom and Dad to let them know I had made it. My friend at Wilson called. She had had a horrible day and had spent the noon hour crying. How our situations reversed! Yesterday she wasn't even worried.

I have just finished reading the children's introductions. They were certainly revealing. The only instruction that I gave the students was the same one I have given to all my classes for years: introduce yourself to me. It has always been customary in my teaching to do this to learn as much as I can as quickly as I can about the students I am to teach. Over the years I have found that these introductions inevitably provoked a response that ran along the same pattern—the number of brothers and sisters, father's occupation, hobbies, and interests. Imagine my surprise then to find that Glenview's seventh graders took an entirely different approach. Instead of routine data about important people in their young lives, Glenview's students turned a critical eye on themselves:

I am very nice to work with. I am not very bad.

My hobby is being on programs. I've never been on television before but I hope some day I will. In the future my only hope in life is being an actor.

Dear Mrs. Culbertson
My name is Lee Roberts and we are glade to have you for a teacher.

It has been nice meating you.

I try to get to school on time. I also make friends easily. I hardly ever get into trouble.

I try to follow all the school rules but someone always make you get out of line.

Sometimes I am bad in clase. I like to work but I am a snow worker. I cannot read very good or spell.

Good morning . . . I will try to do my best because my mother do not like F. So Mrs. Culbison I will work with you I am sure you will work with me.

And I am very nice.

Dear Mrs. Culbertson
Good morning I hope you like teaching us because I think you are a nice teacher a very intellgent. I will not give you any trouble at all.

Mrs. Cubbertson really I hope you get to like me and I hope I get to like you. You seem like a very nice lady. I know I am going to enjoy being under your instructions.

My name is Thomas Lee Moore. But you do not no how proud I am to see you. I want you to know that I like you very much. But I can read very good. I like History very much. And I like Language Art to. But I am pretty good in spelling. Everyone in the class love you. I will not be hard head and do not mind and what you say. I hope you like it very much.

I am known as James Nugent. I am glad to meet you is very nice to me and the class I play a drum and Love History Spelling I Do not like Language too much But I will get my lesson I can't write to will

I can only write will on ink.

To my Lovlest teacher

Your turly
James Nugent
PS. You is a nice teacher

I would like to improve my handwriting in many ways for instance I can't make a r corectly. I like to have test on a topic that I had long ago so that I might improve my thinking ability. Through my years of going to school I was on the honor roll.

I miss my teachers very much because I had gotten use of their ways of teaching but I think if I work hard we will be very friendly throughout the year.

My reading is fair and my spelling is to. I sometimes talk a lot, and sometimes I am quiet. I like all my teachers and I obey them. Most of all I respect them. I also respect my classmates too. My work that I do at school is very neat and I try to write very good to. I am not a lazy student I like to get my work out.

I like coming to school. I will come unless I am sick

or something else bad happen that I can't come to school.
I am not a very smart student I will try to get it.

I am a very intelor younng man I will not give you
any toubl in class roon. I will get my lessun you will not
have to tell me bequite in the class roon and I will be
in on time

I may talk a little bit.

First of all I am a nice little boy and I have noting
against white or color. You like me I like you You treat
me right I treat you right and I do me Homework and
I will obey an get in my seat in the room before the bell
ring. I like everyone out Here and Everyone in the world
all creek and color all but the *devil*.

I am not a bay boy. I come to every day. I has been
absent 4 days.

My mother all way tell me to get a good education.
And attend to good a education.

I eat a lots of sweat. I try to respect my teacher and
fellow study. My best sweat is chocolate.

. . . I try to keep my mertral but I may have to ask my
fellow study for a sheet. I dislike fight. And try to keep
away from agurments, also.

When I lay my head on my desk I don't fill to well.
And I enjoy and like you and prayete you very much. I
will repect you. And I hope we be the best of friend. I
do not provote fight unless I have no chayce. I have good
taste for designs. If you give me a report I will do my best
to try to get a good grade. I try to be intellergate in all
way. And I am selling flower seed I would like for you to
buy some.

I can learn so much.

I don't like to do much work at times and I like to do neet work and not a lot of talking. And I have a good feeling about people and what they do I don't like to set up in my seat because I be tied.

I am good in P.E. that is not all i am good I am good in scone

Good morning Mrs. Culbertson. My name is George. I can Wright a litter I can't read very wall I can do history And I can do a litter of Language. I come to school everyday. I do not be late.

My father is unknown.

All about me.
I can write good with a ink pen. I have clean work. I like History very much. I come to class on time. I do not play in class. I do not eat cookies in class. I can work good. I can make Booket.

I always love to watch TV and eat. But most of all I like when we study the Bible with my mother once a week.

My best friends are God and Jane Henderson.

My parents take our whole family to church every Sunday. Some parents would rather not take their children anywhere because they don't care anything about them. They'd rather buy beer and play dominoes on Sunday's instead of going to church.

In his paper entitled "No Body Like Me," one child wrote:

I am just like all other children. I play and joke with

you. I give you pencil, paper, candy, orange, apple, and things I have sometime at school. I don't fight other peoples and take their lunch. I want steel your paper and pencil, when you is not looking. I don't talk back to the teacher in the room.

> What I Wint you to Know
> I can't sepll to good.
> I can't read too well.
> I can't wirt to well.
> But I wirt to learn.
> I was born in 1957.
> I like to go hun

These tore at my heart strings—especially this last one.

February 18

Another day of turmoil! The high-school teachers got their pink slips today. My friend Randy goes to Peabody. Many of the Timberlane teachers will join us at Glenview.

It was my turn to watch others go through the bitter period I so recently experienced. Furthermore, I was in a Negro school and was able to see the Negro faculty members' reactions to their assignments. One woman was so shocked that she couldn't answer when her name was called. I could sympathize with her. When her name was called a second time, and she still didn't answer, someone said, "Here she is." She still didn't move. Someone took her slip to her.

She was not the only one who was in a state of shock.

Several others seemed to be completely taken aback at receiving transfer assignments. One said that she was not even on the alternate list.

It was interesting to me to see that certain white schools were dreaded assignments to them, just as Glenview had been regarded by those of us at Timberlane.

My students worked well today. I'm trying to find where to start their work. I haven't experienced any hostile reactions to *anything* I've done thus far.

February 19
Today started with a good laugh. When one of the transferees from Timberlane got out of her car, an old Ford with more than one dent in it, she noticed that the big green Cadillac parked next to her still had the lights on. She called to the Negro teacher who owned the car, to stop her before she reached the building. The owner replied, "That's all right. They'll go off in a minute."

I am puzzled because the children, who exhibit such good manners in all other phases of classroom behavior, never reply to me with the "Yes, Ma'am" or "No, Ma'am" that I am accustomed to hearing from students. They say a rather curt "Yes" or "No." I'll wait a few days before I probe into this.

Will I ever learn these children's names? They all look alike to me; I'll never learn to tell them apart. I must find some way to learn their names. I can't teach a child if I can't call his name. I can't keep on asking them to repeat their names.

This may be the easiest teaching I've ever done. They are so far behind the ones I left that I already have stacks of material prepared. Hooray!

February 20

Today I was in the lounge when a Negro teacher said to me, "I hope that you are enjoying your stay in Glenview." I do not know what I might have said to her if I had not been spared an answer by the entry of a group of Negro teachers. One of them was crying, obviously very upset. She was holding a gift that her class had just given her because she was being transferred to a predominantly white school.

"I just can't take it," she sobbed.

Without thinking I said, "Yes, that's just it. None of us wants it, but we have to do it."

She quickly dried her eyes and snapped at me, "Yes, I do want it. I just have to adjust."

Another in the group added, "We've taken it long enough as it is."

The transferee continued, "It will be better for all concerned."

I couldn't resist. "How will it be better?"

"Maybe the whites will realize what we've been doing without for years. It is about time we get equal rights," she replied.

I wasted time thinking about this unpleasant episode when I should have been searching for explanations of the shortage of textbooks and supplies and for a solution to the noise problem.

My desk was empty when I came. So were all of the cabinets. We have plenty of desks, chairs, cabinets, even two nice globes, but no desk supplies. Books are also in short supply. I don't have a single class in which all of the students have textbooks. I have decided what I must do. I am going to take up all of the books and issue them each period before I begin class. At least there will be a book for each one in class that way.

The children don't carry books around with them. They don't use notebooks either. Instead they carry a manila file folder. Very few possess pencils or paper. But they all have cookies!

I cannot figure out the cookie bit. I have never seen so many cookies, so much gum, potato chips, and the like as these Negro children consume. By the time I get to my room, there are cookie wrappers, orange peelings, gum papers—you name it—scattered on the floor. I don't know where the food comes from, but there is certainly plenty of it.

I don't know how all the other transferees are using their lunch period, but several of us from Timberlane take our lunches and meet in my room. I take the Coke bag Mom and Dad brought me. It holds enough crushed ice for a day's supply, plus room for several Cokes and my lunch. The Coke machines at school are never filled, and I have to have my Coke, or my "fix" as Jim calls it.

The noise! The noise! If we could only do something about it. No one who has not heard it would believe it. By the end of the day I am worn out from talking above the loud rumble that never stops. I tried to tape it yesterday to show my family what I meant. However, this is not a problem peculiar to Glenview. One of my telephone buddies says it is the same at Wilson. I'll call her tomorrow to see if they have found a solution.

I should be thankful that within my classroom it is quiet. I couldn't ask for more cooperative students. They're trying hard to please me.

February 20

I talked to my Wilson friend a long time tonight. She said that they have *many* of the same problems, not just noise. They do not have enough textbooks, nor do they have supplies. There are no locks on the cabinets. The flies are eating them up at Wilson. Thank goodness, that's one problem we don't have.

Their children eat all day, as ours do. They stop at neighborhood stores or at vending trucks on the way to school and come into the building with sacks of things to eat or to sell. Also, Wilson and Glenview students keep the school vending machines working overtime.

The Coke machines at Wilson are emptied every night so that they will present no attraction to vandals. Maybe vandals are the reason there are never any Cokes in the machines at Glenview; I don't believe the machines are emptied at night.

This Wilson teacher got some help today with her two main classroom problems. Her Negro supervisor explained that the unbelievable noise is "part of their culture." The "correcting one another" problem stems from their desire to stop any interference with their "good education."

May be true. I don't know. That does help explain

the problems, though. I thought that the "correcting one another" problem was due to the fact that so many have "bossed" younger brothers and sisters that correcting has become a habit.

February 23

I made up my mind during the weekend that I would talk to the children today about manners and my expectations in that area. I asked them why they did not say, "Yes, Ma'am," or "No, Ma'am." They told me that their teachers had told them not to do this, although most of them had been taught at home to address their parents in this manner. I explained that to me this was a small sign of respect that children should give to adults. I expected my own son to show this courtesy. No one showed any objection.

I had intended to talk about the eating before class and the papers on the floor, but there was a noticeable improvement in this area, and I decided I had better leave well enough alone. I did praise them on their progress however.

My school day is settling into a routine. I begin class at 8:10, as we were asked to do, but I lose the first ten minutes to the noise in the hall and outside my window. My class, except for a handful of stragglers, is ready to start on time, for they come to school early. Many arrive as early as 7:15, because their parents leave at that time to go to work. No wonder they are so tired by the end of the day! Others come by bus, and Mr. Hudson hopes that he can get the bus schedule changed so that they won't come so early.

By the way, I knew all the names by Friday. It wasn't a problem after all.

I am not as conscientious about leaving the school as I am about getting there on time. At the first faculty meeting we were told to stay until 3:30, but most of the Negro teachers leave with the children at 3:00, and most of the transferees are close behind them. I have never done anything like this in my life, and I do wish we could have a rule that everyone would keep.

This was crossover day for senior-high teachers. Although I was aware that Kurt had a holiday, I forgot all about it after I got to school, and it was not until afternoon when the transferees came to Glenview that I remembered. In addition to the Timberlane friends, there were several teachers from other schools whom I knew. How good it will be to have a few more white faces around.

The new assistant principal in charge of curriculum, Mrs. Arnold, came today, too. I am looking forward to working with her. I know she is a wonderful worker and a great organizer. I imagine that she was one of the "some" that Mr. Wheat meant when he said, ". . . some were strong in certain areas, and that assisted us in using criteria to invite them to assist us." Naturally, there had to be some crossovers among the administrators, too.

February 24

Our lunch group transferred from my classroom to the home-ec department today, as two home-ec teachers were among the transferees. I have to laugh at myself when I think about how I tried to console them and give them assurance that we would make it. It comforted them to know that I left my tear-gas gun at home after the first couple of days. Has one week changed me that much? I'm not the only one. One of our junior-high teachers had been hospitalized with ulcers before the move, but I heard him assuring several of the newcomers that it was by no means an impossible situation.

I'll agree that it isn't impossible, but we do have a long way to go. Although only a week (it seems more like a month) has passed, I have drawn some conclusions about my group. Spelling is a big problem. Apparently, these children have not had formal spelling lessons. They are also poor readers. They are word-callers; they do not understand what they are reading. However, they write well. Their penmanship is far better than I expected to find. In addition, their time concept in history is much better than I dreamed it would be.

I got a message from our school-board-member friend today. He said that he had been out to Clinton and the grounds *were* in bad shape. He didn't know what had happened; maybe some weekend party-makers had left the trash.

February 24

Since I've been teaching school, I have loaned many things and I have borrowed a few, but this is the first school in which I have had students come to the room to borrow the pencil sharpener. I had not properly appreciated the small blessing of having a pencil sharpener in my room. Students from throughout the wing come to my room to sharpen their pencils.

The lack of such small items is irritating to the transferees, who are not used to this. We feel certain that these schools were issued ample supplies; what has happened to them?

When I went to the office to ask the principal for supplies, he told me, "Keep Magic Markers in your purse. Don't dare let them get to the students. They'll mark anything with them. They just love Magic Markers."

In order to have scissors, tape, paper clips, tacks, and pencils, I have to store them in my purse. The desk doesn't lock; the metal supply cabinet doesn't lock; I don't have a key to my door. I have never locked my desk before, and only twice have I lost appreciable amounts of supplies during my eighteen years of teaching—once to a summer break-in at the school and the other while a substitute was teaching for me.

Vandalism must be quite a serious problem here. Otherwise, how could a teacher put up with the inconvenience of carrying desk supplies around with her? These small items are things that I use every day of the week, almost every hour. I even take my own stapler, which the Negroes call a "stapling machine," back and forth from home.

The one supply that does appear to be present in abundance is the chalkboard eraser. I say this because apparently everyone had a habit of using my cinder block wall to dust erasers. I couldn't stand to see that unsightly wall any longer, so today I took old rags and detergent with me, but I didn't let the children see them. I gave them a pep talk about taking pride in their room. It was successful. I had so many volunteers that I couldn't use all of them. Two boys chose to miss their "break" to contine cleaning. Now the walls are spotless, and we will keep them that way.

As the youngsters were cleaning, they talked among themselves, and I made an observation that was surprising to me. It was suddenly obvious that these students have no idea that most of the white teachers are here against their will. With many, it is a matter of having to keep their jobs. Some would have preferred to resign rather than transfer and would have done so if they could have found other work, but these children are unaware of these facts.

Just when I think that I'm ready to concentrate all my thoughts on Glenview, something happens to pull my world apart. A nice letter came from the principal of Timberlane:

Dear Mrs. Culbertson:

I would like very much for you to know how much I personally appreciated your many efforts and countless hours spent at Timberlane.

I remember a supervisor stating that she could tell how talented a teacher was from the appearance of her room. I can honestly say that your room gave the appearance of so many fine things being accomplished and then, of course, the comments of boys and girls cannot be overlooked. I sincerely mean it when I say I never heard anything but the best from your students, including my own son.

February 25

"May I speak?"

This simple question has nearly driven us transferees out of our minds. The pattern seems to have developed in the Negro schools so that this question is not a question at all but part of a ritual, repeated over and over in every classroom.

I have learned that the door to the classroom may open without warning at any time. Invariably, a student from another class will glance at me and go into his routine: "May I speak?" To startled intruders in my classroom I have been saying, "I am sorry. We are having class now. You will have to visit with your friends during your break time." So far the response has been courteous. One girl "accidentally" let the door close harder than was necessary, but I consider that minor. I told the children to spread the word that I do not permit "speaking" during class, and my flow of visitors has dwindled to a trickle.

Children are not the only ones who burst into the room unannounced. A friend at another school told me that right in the middle of a class the door was pushed open, and a loud-mouthed woman yelled, "John Henry!" No one replied, and she repeated the call. She then turned to the dumbfounded teacher and asked if John Henry were present. When she was told that he was not present, she left without another word.

The students' observations of us sometimes startle me. One boy told me today, "All white teachers can't control children. There's one who says, 'Please be quiet. Oh, please be quiet.' Why, no one can even hear him begging." Then with a sharp eye on me, he continued, "He's going to have to learn that you can't get Negroes to mind that way."

I'm sleeping again. I haven't been nauseated since the day of the transfer. If I had only listened to that guy who said something like ninety percent of what we worry

about never happens, think of the agony I would have
avoided.

February 26

Customs that have developed in the
Negro schools absolutely baffle us white teachers. The
M&S orders—Materials and Supplies—are a chore that we
are accustomed to doing on our own time, usually at
home at night. We discovered that this wasn't the case in
the Negro schools. At one elementary school there was a
teachers' meeting, and everybody worked on the orders
together. This would be fine after school, but it wasn't
done that way. The meeting was held during school, and
the students stayed in the room unattended, while teachers planned for the coming year.

At another school the teachers were told to put an
assignment on the board and go to a meeting. The teachers there learned that this practice was always followed.
When the children completed the assignment, they were
free to play.

At another school two Negro teachers sewed on sewing machines in their classroom all day while the students
worked?? The teachers called out spelling, gave instructions, and took care of routine matters while they made
costumes for PTA programs. Miraculous!

I think that this type of thing, more than any other,
accounts for the slow progress in learning in these schools.
So much teaching time is wasted! In the white schools we
felt obliged to make every minute count for every pupil,
and this usually meant different kinds and amounts of
work for each pupil.

I have worked on my M&S order tonight. I am ordering the things that I would use if I were here. I hope I am
not. I have heard many remarks about things being un-
equal, but I know one thing for sure that's equal: The
amount of money per pupil that I am allotted at Glenview is exactly the same as I had at Timberlane.

Since I had an opportunity to get supplies each of the
three years at Timberlane, I had accumulated the basic
desk and room supplies, and I would be ordering extras.
Glenview has been open for many years and should be in
a better position than Timberlane regarding supplies,
but I am having to order basics.

Wasting money replacing "lost" supplies annoys me,
but that's not the only thing that does. I continue to be
annoyed by the constant eating that goes on. Once a
home-ec teacher, always a home-ec teacher, I guess. To see
children who need nourishing meals and balanced diets
constantly chewing on "junk" just makes me sick. My
students have learned not to throw the wrappers and
peelings on the floor, but they haven't stopped eating—
not entirely, anyway.

My past experiences give me some understanding of
this eating problem. When I taught in Texas, I had to
deal with a very similar situation. I was in an all-white
school where there were two distinct, widely separated
economic groups—not black and white, but the rice grow-
ers' children and the pumpers' children. The pumpers'
children behaved in the same manner as the Glenview
children. They ate junk all the time. They didn't bring
supplies to my home-ec class, but they found plenty of
money for knicknacks to eat.

In complete despair over the situation, I went to the

principal for help. He said to me, "If you had not had any candy or other treats but had watched other children enjoying them, what would you do if you had a nickel to spend? You'd do just what these youngsters do."

I'm sure he was right, but it's still distressing to me.

February 27

I am down in the dumps tonight, and this worries me because I thought I had adjusted. I do just fine until some former student calls and he says he isn't learning anything or that everything's loused up. Poor kids! Adjusting to a new teacher with new methods in the middle of the year is hard. After seeing firsthand the pace at which work is carried on at Glenview, I'm sure that it is much too slow for many of my former pupils. But many of the calls I get are from children who have trouble learning; the slower pace isn't enough.

I know what has given me the blues. I received this note today:

> Dear Mrs. Culbertson,
>
> Our family wanted you to know how sorry we are about your transfer, and especially we want to thank you for the years with John and Melanie. I am so thankful that we were able to have you and that marvelous class for the time we did.

I guess I'm all too human. I do like a kind word, and I like to know that my efforts are appreciated. This note was such a contrast to the attitude voiced by one of my Negro boys this morning. A group of boys was standing around before the bell rang, and Frederick was fussing about one of his men teachers.

"You just have to behave," said a friend.

Frederick looked at me, not his friend, and replied, "White teachers are as mean as Negro teachers. They don't use the same way to be mean though. The Negroes use a stick, but the whites are strict without a stick. They won't let you do anything."

The children standing around nodded their heads vigorously in agreement. One said, "I didn't know teachers could be so strict without a whip." This critical analysis of the new white teachers continued.

I had heard similar remarks before. Apparently Negro children didn't realize that teachers ever came to the classroom without a stick.

Frederick added one other revealing statement: "We used to play radios and record players at school and have fun. Now all we do is work."

There have been very few comments about the teachers—pro or con—but one student wrote in a paragraph about her general dislikes: "One thing I don't like is when a teacher loud talks me."

My classes are shaping up nicely. Almost all are in the room when the bell rings, and the food problem is vanishing fast. I haven't seen a sign of any objections about what I'm doing, but one of my friends at another school got a note from one of her eighth graders that said that the teacher was too "damned strict." I'm glad that I don't have that type of student. It's easy to work with these appreciative students, and it would be difficult to work with belligerent ones.

March

March 1

     I made up my mind tonight that I'm going back tomorrow and get my youngsters on the road to some real learning. We are going to bridge some of those terrible gaps that are handicapping them.

My first-period class has two distinct groups: the "cans" and the "cannots." About half the group falls into each category. The "cannot" level ranges from primer to fifth grade. The others can keep up with seventh-grade material but are weak in critical thinking and spelling, especially.

My fourth-period class really has its problems. For one thing, they want to stay out with their friends for a second lunch period, so some of them invariably do. It is always harder to get any group of students to settle down after lunch period. This group has two strikes against it because of the hour of the day. For some reason they are scheduled to me for history but not for English. They need spelling desperately, but I can't do it all—especially in one hour per day. They need a two-hour "block" badly.

My last block is by far the best group I have. They are jewels. I have never taught a sweeter, nicer, better-behaved class. Almost all of them can do the work. If I had had them all year, I would have them ready for the eighth grade.

No two classes are ever alike in any school. These follow the same pattern. I'll have to handle each class differently.

March 2

Today I had a heart-to-heart talk with the students. I told them that I had observed that reading and spelling were their greatest weaknesses and that "book detective" work and handwriting were their finest assets. They really are the most amazing "book detectives." They can find the answer to anything. This seems strange to me, for I am used to "I can't find the answer. What page is it on? I need help." Many white students ask for help before they honestly try to find an answer. Not these. They don't ask for help—ever.

We decided on a course of study. I grouped them for spelling today, and I hope to work out some kind of grouping for reading. I see now that my careful packing was in vain. I will be using my reading materials after all.

I asked the children to write some of their reactions to the changes that have occurred during the past two weeks. I was pleased to find that most of them were reacting favorably. Typical comments were:

> Mrs. Cuberson is the type who enjoy having fun during the time she spends with us. She also takes time explaining things to do. Now I knows that I am going to have fun with her.

> I cannot spell well because in over classes I don't have a chance to spell.

I like my new teacher very much and I miss my old teacher very much.

I miss Mrs. Jones so very much but I have learned a lot from her the pass two weeks.

I would like you to know that i need a little help on my reading because i am planning on being a nice teacher just like my new teacher she is one of the most nicest teacher you could ever dream of. . .

The senior-high white transferees in an all-Negro school were furious last week when the Afro-American Club displayed several bulletin boards showing black militants with guns on their shoulders and presenting pictures of well-known Negro militant leaders. "We dig Mohammed Ali" was the caption on one of the boards. After the white teachers complained to the principal, the material was removed.

It has been such a pleasant surprise to find that this type of thing isn't going on here!

March 3

I took up all of the textbooks and decided to issue what I needed when I needed them. We are trying hard to recover all the books we can. I gave a good pep talk to the students and asked them to look at home for books. "If you will just bring them in and put them on the cabinet, there won't be any questions asked," I said.

"I can't bring all mine back in one trip," one youngster said.

I suggested that he bring a few each day until he had brought all of them.

I wonder how many books will show up. The books have to be somewhere. It was reported in a faculty meeting the other day that $7,000 had been spent on books for Glenview since September, but everyone is complaining that he has no textbooks. There is a terrible shortage.

I can see some of the reasons. There was no system whatsoever in the initial issuance of books. No check was made of which book was issued to which student. If a student loses his book, he simply takes the first one he finds and writes his name in it. I wonder whether they ever pay for a lost or damaged book. I have no book records by which to check them in at the end of school.

And the books that we do have are messy and dirty. Magic Markers have been used to decorate them. I would capitalize on their love for doodling and decorating and have a bookcover-decorating contest, if we had time. Paper sacks could be used, so there wouldn't be any expense to amount to anything. Maybe the books would stay cleaner then, but I don't have the time. . . .

My mother's comments were interesting. She recalled the day when she was rearing her own children, and Huey Long was elected governor with the promise of free school books for everyone. "I remember when free school books were first issued. It seemed very complicated at first, and we refused to accept them. We bought your sisters' books. But, as it turned out, it wasn't so bad after all. Parents and students learned how to take care of the books or pay for lost ones, and the Negroes will have to do the same." Very interesting. . . .

I have discovered, too, that it isn't just textbooks that are missing. The library has suffered from the students' careless regard of books.

When I read the information concerning the library procedures at Glenview, I was delighted. It sounded as if I would be able to get a lot of help there. With this in mind, I assigned a book report due at the end of the six weeks. This has been a standard procedure for my English classes.

When I went to lunch, I commented to some of the teachers that my classes were excited about doing a rebus book report because they had never done one. I also showed them some of the excellent practice stories the students had done to get the knack of substituting pictures for words.

"Where are they going to get the books to read?" Joan asked, rather strangely, I thought.

"In the library," I answered.

"I don't think there are eighty books down there that seventh graders could read," she said.

I was sick. I pictured the beautiful shelves of books at Timberlane and recalled how eagerly my seventh-graders there used the library. It was not unusual to see many of them leave on Friday with two books to read during the weekend.

"What has happened to the books?" I asked. "I am sure they get the same allotment for books that other schools do."

"I don't know," Joan said, "but I can guess. I imagine the same thing has happened to library books that happens to textbooks. When the children take them home, they consider the books their property and don't bother to bring them back. I heard that one elementary school lost 1500 books last year."

I know how my free period will be spent tomorrow.

I'll be "free" to do what I have to do—memorize those library shelves. There won't be time to go to the lounge to grade papers, relax a minute, and get *that Coke.*

March 4

I went to the library this morning, and I am sorry to say that Joan is right. If I were doing a history paper for college, I could find plenty of reference material. But I didn't find ten books of fiction suitable for my classes. I'll have to write off the Glenview library.

Fortunately, I was able to call on some friends and scare up a few books this afternoon. Kurt and his friends contributed a collection of classic comic books. I have about twenty hardback books to start my classroom collection. I also have a literature sampler kit that a friend contributed to the cause. Joan has promised to bring some magazines. This is a good start.

While I was chasing around collecting books this afternoon, I stopped to visit a minute with one of my former co-workers from Timberlane. When the junior-high transfers were made, she received several new Negro students. They were far behind her class of seventh graders at Timberlane; so she issued fifth-grade readers to them. She thought this would be a good time to do something to help Walter, a Negro student whom she had all year and who was far behind the class. She issued him a reader along with the others.

Suddenly, instead of the cooperative, pleasant boy he had been, Walter became sullen, even hostile. Finally she asked him what was wrong.

"My daddy wants to know why you *sot* me back."

"Walter, you were having some problems with regular work, and I thought I would help you catch up."

He thought a minute and then blurted out, "I wants to catch up, but I don't want to catch up with *them!*"

That same identity problem arose wherever students were mixed. The "old" Negro students already in the school did not want to mix with the "new" Negro students coming into the school.

Here it is 9:30 a.m., and I'm just getting ready to do the routine school work for tomorrow. I didn't get in from my "collections" tour until late, and, as usual, two hungry mouths were waiting. It's so late, and I should get busy immediately with that set of papers, but I keep thinking about what an eye-opener this experience has already been.

By this time, at Glenview—and it is the same with friends transferred to other Negro schools—the transferees are wondering what the school board and administrators in the central office and state department were doing to let Negroes get in this predicament. Where was the supervision? Why weren't the standards for the schools the same? I'm not talking about the brick buildings; both groups have their share of architectural masterpieces. That's just it! The real situation was hidden. The outside appearances have given the impression that the Negroes were receiving a "separate but equal" education. It is obvious to most of us now that they were not.

A lot of it has probably been from forces beyond anyone's control, but at least someone should have known the true state of things in the Negro schools. Nobody in the profession did, I guess—that is, nobody who could do anything about it. And certainly the general public didn't know. School board members are reported as saying that the crossover has opened the eyes of everyone. (Or will, I'd think!)

Maybe the Negroes put their best foot forward, didn't complain, and appeared to be handling their own situations so well that the school board blindly accepted things on face value. Apparently, many of the Negroes were not aware of their own limitations and problems and did not realize that they needed help. Although identical instructions have been given to the administrators at joint meetings, they were not used the same—maybe the instructions had different meanings to the Negroes.

Or was it wishful thinking that the Negroes had an equal education that kept anyone from rocking the boat?

During the weeks of agony that preceded the crossover, I never once pictured the Negro schools as they really are!

March 5
                    The children were so excited about "our library." I let some of the boys go out to my car and bring in the boxes. I let them examine everything and then we set up a system for checking the books out for use.

This was a day I had been dreading in history, for we have been studying about American wars and had come to the Civil War. Sure enough, there was a moment I will long remember. We had been discussing the abolitionists, and one of the girls said, "Mrs. Culbertson, would you have been an abolitionist?"

I thought about that one. Then I said, "It is hard to say what we would have done if we had lived back then.

I would probably have been a poor farmer in the South and wouldn't have owned any slaves." That satisfied her, and the lesson continued.

Sometimes I think they ask me questions just to see how I will react. The other day a boy asked me, "What color is God?"

I swallowed hard before I said, "God is different things to different people. Each of us has his own image of God. Your image and mine may not be the same."

He didn't pursue the question. I think he was testing me to see if I would say that God was white.

Some of them, like Frederick, know how to make their questions into jokes that don't offend or challenge. There are three in the room who like to joke about the black-white situation, but Frederick is the only one who can do it with the expertness of a Flip Wilson. One of the girls had brought a picture of her little sister, a pigtailed eight- or nine-year-old. She dropped it in the room, and I had put it on the corner of my desk so that I would re-member to return it to her.

Frederick walked by my desk and saw the picture. He picked it up, pretended to study it carefully, and turned to me. "Is this your daughter?" he asked.

I burst out laughing, and all of the class joined me. He said, "You know, I just thought you brought a picture of your child to show us."

March 5
                    I have to move again, just when I'm getting settled, but this time it's just one cabinet. Marian called this afternoon to say, "I hate to ask you to come get

your cabinet you left in my room, but my room is bursting at the seams, and I need the space. You know, since Timberlane has gained over 300 new students, my classes have swelled so that I have one with thirty-seven."

I shouldn't have had to be reminded that she needed the space. Since Clinton High School closed, many of those students were sent to Timberlane, and I've been hearing about all the problems they've created. Besides, I lost some from Glenview who had to transfer to Timberlane. Maybe Timberlane's gains didn't impress me as much as its losses, since some good friends' children were among the six whites scheduled to leave Timberlane for a Negro school, and I've been hearing about all the problems the family has encountered in enrolling the children in a private school.

March 6

I am trying hard to teach a second-grade spelling list to some of my students. Today I called out "think" and a little later I came to "thank." A student told me that I had already called that word. He didn't hear the difference between the two words. That is one of the problems with their spelling. They do not enunciate clearly, and they do not hear the differences between many vowel sounds. They try to spell the words the way they hear them pronounced and, sad but true, they've heard them mispronounced all of their lives.

This boy's spelling could cause the reader to get an entirely different message.

The Habit I tried to break was to stop play with my figure. Everyday I played with my figure. I was 5 years old when I started playing with my figure. I get a string and I rip it off a towel. I play with it. My grandfather put moss on my hand. I took it off. I went to the bathroom and wash it off. And I was playing with it right on. My grandfather put some pepper on my hand. I went into the bathroom another I wash it except I throught I did. My grandparent did not like me playing with my figure. I put it in my mouth. It was hot started ran and crying.

Figure—finger?

An interesting incident occurred at fourth period today. I let my class into the room at 12:02. Since I am the only teacher who has a class in that wing at fourth period, no one is supposed to enter except my students. Today a boy slipped in and refused to leave when I told him to do so. I asked the class to tell me who the boy was. One of my students said, "Jesse Stuart." The snickers of the other children confirmed my suspicion that he had given me the first name that popped into his head. I asked the class if they thought it was right to protect someone who was doing wrong. I pointed out that I had trusted them before, but now, after this, I wasn't too sure how I would feel. They were all a part of the attempt to deceive me. They responded quickly, and everyone tried to tell me the name of the offender.

We continued a discussion of honesty. I told them how impressed I had been when a fifth-period student turned in a quarter she had found on her desk. When the student who had left it returned, I was able to give him his money.

"She was crazy for turning it in!" one exclaimed.

And the class agreed one hundred percent!

All was not lost today. One of the men teachers who came to Glenview from Timberlane began organizing a system for the distribution of books. Hooray for him! He did this at Timberlane, and we had a most efficient system. He will take up all books not in use and begin numbering them. I consider this a big step forward.

March 10
                    School bells mean nothing to these students at Glenview. Tardy slips, admits—things like that are unimportant. Ten minutes after the class bell rings, the halls are full of students milling around. They completely disregard the bell.

I expect my students to get to class on time, and they are rarely late. They lose their "break"—recess time—if they are late. I have decided that teaching them the value of punctuality will be an accomplishment.

A friend who worked with the Head Start program one summer was battling this same problem of tardiness. She came up with the idea of having a Kool-Aid party every morning. A child who was tardy missed the refreshments. I'm sure that worked if her children loved refreshments the way these do. But what child needs Kool-Aid for breakfast?

Much of the tardiness is caused by a lack of routine in their homes. They go to bed whenever they choose. Most of my students talk about the late movies on television. I have made a ruling that they cannot put their heads on their desks because so many were catching up on their lost sleep that way. Someone told me that the putting heads down is an escape mechanism, but I do not agree. It is late movies! One friend says she can't have class on Tuesday because many of her students go to the wrestling matches on Monday night. Wow!

March 11

Disturbing news greeted us in the lounge this morning. One of the Negro teachers went back to Glenview last night to help with a program. When she went out to get into her car to go home, she found it jacked up with all of the tires gone.

Something else is disturbing! Those of us who transferred are perplexed about the difference between the number of students actually attending class and the number on the class roll. Many are beginning to talk about padded lists. Some of the teachers have students on their rolls that they have yet to see, and the year is nearly gone. They don't even bother to report them as absentees any more.

I can account for almost all of mine. Four I have never seen, but the assistant principal told me that one is in jail, one is in reform scshool, and another comes to school but just doesn't go to classes! He doesn't know the whereabouts of the fourth.

Mr. Hudson told us not to drop anyone unless the visiting teacher notified us to do so. I wonder why the names are kept on the rolls. I've never seen anything like this in a white school. Pupil accounting doesn't seem to be important. The teacher enrollment form that we fill out at the beginning of the year for the census had always been *the* nightmare form of the year. Every "i" had to be dotted, and every "t" had to be crossed. If you made a mistake, you started over. It was not accepted in the office until it was perfect. The one that I found in my desk has spaces left blank, names crossed out, and corrections scratched in on every other item!

March 12

My "free" period was spoiled today by a militant young Negro teacher who had found an audience in the lounge. She was supposed to be with her class, but she was entertaining a group of Negroes with tales of her experiences in a white school. Her talk went like this: "That school was horrible. You wouldn't believe what happened to me there. Why, the parents threatened me so that the FBI had to escort me home every day. The principal kept telling me that I didn't understand the white students. He said that I was teaching in a poverty area. I didn't say anything, but I thought, 'Don't tell me anything about poverty. I *know* about poverty. . .' "

She went on to tell about being mistreated in another school, that one in another state. Surely there must be a message somewhere in two experiences of the same nature. I kept thinking that if she didn't get down the hall and see about her class, she might have a third experience!

A boy said to me today, "White teachers don't handle the students like Negro teachers do. Our Negro teacher either whipped us or sent us outside."

"I'll bet you liked getting sent outside," I commented.

"No, that was worse than a whipping. Then you had

to dodge the assistant principal and the principal. If *they* caught you outside, you were really in trouble."

There was more noise than ever today, and it was from the class of a white transferee. This teacher had had trouble before coming to Glenview, so the disturbance in the room didn't surprise me. What did surprise me was that the Negro staff at the school seemed to be embarrassed that a white teacher was failing in the handling of the students.

None of the Negroes has commented, but, judging from their expressions, I think they are making discoveries, too. They are shocked to discover that white teachers are just like Negro teachers—some good ones and some weak ones.

It seems to me that at Glenview problems with discipline have nothing to do with the color, size, or sex of the teacher. It doesn't seem to matter in the least. My friends at other schools agree it is the same everywhere.

March 13

Mr. Hudson issued a policy statement about dress for all students today. Girls must wear socks. Boys must wear belts and have their shirttails tucked in.

Five minutes later one of my boys walked in with his shirttail out. I told him to tuck it in. He walked to the back of the room, unzipped his trousers, and tucked his shirt in. He came back and sat down without a word. No one in the room except me seemed to think that anything unusual had gone on. I couldn't imagine a white boy unzipping his pants before a class of students.

I mentioned this to a counselor later in the day. She said, "Why, he didn't think a thing about that. If you had grown up in one room with a big family, you would have lost all modesty, too."

"Then tell me why they don't buckle their belts."

"That's simple. They leave the belt unbuckled so that they can whip it out for a weapon should the need arise suddenly."

"Is there an explanation for the untied shoelaces?"

"That's just easiest, I guess."

Anyway, I'm learning.

I keep wondering how my Glenview students would fare if they had to attend a mixed school. How would they make out socially? White girls, even the seventh graders, haven't been wearing socks for years. They wear hose, and they wouldn't be caught dead in tennis shoes. Yet here socks and tennis shoes are regular classroom dress.

The boys, too, might have trouble making the grade with their safety-pin-closed pants. I have never seen so many big safety pins before. Zippers pull apart because pants are frequently outgrown and too tight. So a pin holds the gap together. Very few have matching colors and designs in their clothes. Most of the clothes came from rummage sales conducted by white church or school groups. Some of the students dress well enough by any standards, but this is more often true in the upper high-school grades. There are some flashy dressers among that group—orange or purple pants, flowered shirts, etc.

These who can afford the latest fashions will probably fare rather well in the white schools, but many are going to have difficulty, I'm afraid. Apparently some are already having trouble. One Negro maid told someone that it is taking everything that she can make to dress her children for "white" school.

The teachers' clothes are in contrast. The Negro teachers are beautifully dressed, especially the men. Everything matches—shirts, ties, handkerchiefs.

The number of skilled seamstresses among the Negro faculty members and secretarial staff is probably the highest of any school in the country. They aren't mediocre seamstresses either. They use the finest details, and latest materials and patterns to make clothes that have a "store-bought" appearance.

March 16

Frederick bounced into the room, snapping his fingers and grinning mischievously from ear to ear. "I composed a song about you this weekend. Do you want to hear it?"

He twisted and danced and sang. At first I could hear "Mrs. Culbertson" this and "Mrs. Culbertson" that, but when he came to the end of his song, he changed it to "Cubby."

"Cubby's my baby," he sang, snapping his fingers. "Cubby's my baby."

March 17

I'm learning a new language at Glenview. "In the woods" is a new answer to roll call that I now understand. Woodland adjoins the school, and some students ride the bus to and from school but prefer to jump the fence and spend the day in the woods. Often the parents are totally unaware that the child is not attending school regularly. When the name of such a student is called, others speak up matter-of-factly, answering, "In the woods," or "He's shooting hookey."

James is a "woods" boy, it seems. The few days he has attended my classes he has undoubtedly been miserable. He is so far behind even the weakest ones that some make fun of him. I talked it over with the class today to explain how James must feel toward "poking fun," and they agreed to treat James more kindly if we can get him to come back to school. Several boys volunteered to try.

Another thing that I am learning here is that some school children do not complain about cafeteria food. I haven't heard a Glenview student complain. That's very unusual! I understand that at one Negro elementary school there are no complaints or scraps either. Obviously, these children love the food! One boy wrote, "The food be good and I like to eat."

I'm also discovering that the students are wondering about me.

Very seriously today one of the girls came up to me after class and asked, "Are you rich?"

"No," I replied, "Why do you ask?"

"Because you have been so many places we study about and you wear pretty clothes."

I told her, "I have worked and saved my money to be able to travel. When I was your age, I didn't get to travel. I've done all of my traveling since I have been married, and I make my own clothes."

She calmly said, "Oh, some of us wondered."

I wonder what else they wonder?

Absenteeism plagues me. You can't teach students who aren't at school, and these have such a casual attitude toward class attendance that missing a day—or a week—doesn't seem to matter to most of them. Regular attendance for a student is unusual. Excuses vary: "I had to pay the bills"—"I had to take care of my sister's children"—"My mother was in a wreck, and there's no one to take care of her."

We try to get excuses brought from home, but that appears impossible. To begin with, many of the parents can't read and write.

One excuse I can't figure out is "no shoes." They are in school one day with shoes and are absent the next day or two because they don't have shoes. That one ranks with an elementary transferee's student who said he had to be absent to take care of his mother's children.

"Aren't they your sisters and brothers?"

"Oh, yes'um."

Teacher absenteeism plagues the principals, I know. Last Friday, there were fifteen out of seventy-eight absent at Glenview. Another Friday, there were thirteen teachers absent, and the absentees are from both groups—the blacks and the whites. Many white transferees are taking every day of sick leave that they have left. One friend told me, "A four-day work week is all I can take. It takes three days instead of two for me to regain my energy to face this frustrating confusion."

I'm sorry that the teachers aren't setting better examples for the students. I've always believed that old adage, "What you do speaks so loudly that I can't hear what you say."

I was just thinking about some conclusions I've

drawn about attendance. When I taught accelerated students, I found absenteeism was extremely low. There had to be a real reason for one of them to miss school. It's the same old question: "Which comes first?" Do they attend school because they are good students, or are they good students because they attend school?

March 18

What a day I had today! So much on my mind. It wasn't students, it wasn't black or white—just an old allergy to smoke. There is a car-wrecking yard near Glenview, and today was the day for burning old cars. I've taught with dripping nose, red eyes, queasy stomach and a headache.

Frederick saved the day. "Mrs. Culbertson, why does your nose turn red?" Then before I could answer, he chortled gleefully, "Mine don't!"

Some strange differences show up. Who can explain them? A commerce teacher has so many boys taking shorthand she is astounded. She never had a boy student before in a white class. In the black school, she has almost as many boys as girls. I wonder where they are going to use shorthand—maybe in college.

Her typing students are hunting and pecking and writing one letter per period. (A good student should type about four in the same time.) The students are so slow, according to the teacher, because they had not learned the right method. Though since they have learned to erase properly and clean around the typewriters, the room and the typewriters stay cleaner. She wonders how much progress they would have made if they had been using the proper methods all along.

The Glenview faculty has a custom of sending flowers to funerals, but the white members of the faculty are never asked to contribute.

A girl came into the classroom one morning last week to ask the class to contribute to a "floral" for a high-school girl's mother. None of my students knew her, so she didn't get any money from them. Today a student asked me to contribute to a fund for someone. I asked her the name, etc. "I don't know exactly who it is, but I heard about her from someone. . . "

I wonder if the central office knows that these student collections go on. I thought that sort of thing was taboo.

March 19

Lack of supplies is still a handicap, but things may improve in that area. I read in the paper that the school board has approved Mr. Wheat's order for new supplies. "$100,000.00 expenditure for textbooks, materials and supplies to replace those which School Superintendent Herbert Wheat said are 'missing' due to mismanagement. Wheat said that books and supplies were found to be missing when teachers transferred at mid-term. He blamed the shortages on mismanagement at the school level or 'lack of youngsters caring. Whatever the reason,' he said, 'it must be corrected.' "

It rained today, and Glenview campus was flooded. There weren't many students present. Absenteeism is always high, but it is worse on rainy days. Bad houses, inadequate clothing, bad roads, I guess.

March 20

One of the home-ec teachers, who transferred with the senior-high bunch, has a unique problem. Students keep coming to her department to buy cookies. She keeps telling them, "I don't have any." It seems that it was the custom before the February change for the home-ec department to keep cookies for sale.

The eating problem is something! Today I noticed an indirect carryover into some English writings the students had done. The majority described July 4th—not December 25th—as their favorite holiday. The reason— lots of food for picnics!

Today while the lunch gang ate sandwiches and chips, we unintentionally summarized some of the things we've learned in these few weeks. We agreed that slow-learner techniques work best—change material often because of their short attention span, use many different devices (especially audio-visual aids), use oral reading, give longer time to finish work, apply little or no pressure, and increase the amount of work gradually.

I don't know who's being educated, but I believe it's the white teachers.

March 23

News of a gang fight at the school was unsettling. I didn't see it, but the news traveled fast into the classrooms. The police came and took some boys away.

Mr. Hudson said that most of the ones involved didn't attend Glenview or any other school. This brings up another problem at Glenview. Visitors on the grounds are very common. It seems that they are former students or older boys and girls simply looking for a place to go. They are referred to as "outsiders." The school has been their cultural center for so long, that they use the grounds for a meeting place. I am reminded of the time when I was in elementary school and visitors were very common. Cousins, older or younger sisters and brothers, et al., visited even in classrooms. I remember sitting in the desk seat with another child all day to give a guest a seat. It has been a long time since I've heard of visitors being allowed in white schools, though.

The police come by rather often. It is no longer surprising to look out of the window to see a police car drive up on the grounds between the wings of the building. The principal, assistant principal, and some other male teachers keep in touch with one another with intercom sets. But, generally speaking, the discipline is much better than I expected. Some individual teachers fail to control their classes, as is true in other schools, and naturally there are the occasional discipline problems that all teachers—even the super ones—have to face. Yet the children don't misbehave to any unusual degree when they are in the halls or on the grounds.

The design of the Glenview building creates some problems. The open windows at eye level are too tempting to many a youngster. They just can't resist the urge to call to their friends when they pass by. Also the friends outside laughing and talking are disturbing. Their favorite places to "visit" seem to be the "off-limits" areas between the wings.

Certainly, I find Glenview much noisier than the white schools I have known. All of the white teachers in the Negro schools comment on this above all else. Even moving desks and chairs, tapping pencils, shuffling feet, and humming are done with no restraint and contribute heavily to the overall noise that makes the necessary quiet environment for learning out of the question.

The visitors, fights, and noise apparently aren't keeping the teachers from teaching because Mr. Hudson seems well pleased with the way things are going. Today in faculty meeting, he said, "Whatever y'all are doing, keep it up. This is better than average."

March 24

"Do any of you know anything about Myradell Jones? She hasn't been here since I've been here, but her name is on the roll."

The entire class burst into delighted laughter.

Someone volunteered, "Mrs. Culbertson, Myradell just had a baby."

Another voice added, "Yeah, and Norman is the daddy."

I looked up to see Norman beaming happily while everyone else laughed.

"Tell her about it, Norman," said Charlie.

I quickly changed the subject to the history lesson and Reconstruction. My past teaching experience never prepared me for the multiple love affairs of these seventh graders. In the white schools, the average seventh-grade boy still thinks of girls as poison—or at least a nuisance. Usually, there is a more mature boy or two, or one who has been retained, who'll have a girl—but at Glenview almost every girl has a boy friend, and most of the boys have several girl friends. I have picked up notes being passed to young sweethearts—"soul lovers"—that make me blush.

March 26

Well, here it is spring, and at Glenview we don't have one problem that turned up as regularly as spring in the white schools. The white students' version of flirting is very mild it seems. That is the frolic the boys have this time of year taking the girls' purses. The girls love it and squeal and chase boys all day. I know at Timberlane and Kirby and elsewhere they're wishing the sap wouldn't rise so high just this year, but here at Glenview we don't have that.

To begin with, the girls don't carry purses—at least not many seventh graders do. They don't bother as much with make-up either. It is the boys who are constantly preening themselves at Glenview. They seem to like combing their hair all the time—so much so, that I made a rule that hair combing cannot go on during my classes. In fact, combs must be kept hidden. Most of the boys keep their huge combs in their back pockets but only because they are not allowed to keep them stuck in their hair.

I laughed at my friend, Randy. She thought the big curved-handled combs used for Afro haircuts were switchblades because all that is visible is the curved handles. They aren't switchblades, but apparently they make good weapons—especially the metal ones that can be sharpened. Some schools have had to outlaw metal combs and cake cutters, but I don't think that Glenview has had this problem.

I wonder how this Negro teacher is adjusting to the

Afro haircuts. Diane wrote this about one of her elementary teachers: "One teacher I don't like is Mrs. Brown. She has a rule that I don't like. It is that she doesn't like for your hair to be curled."

Preference forms came out last week. They have already been returned, and I don't believe there were many white teachers who asked to return to Glenview. Most of the white teachers did say that if they had to return to a predominantly Negro school, they would choose Glenview. I know one who said that she had been so frustrated this year that she wants to come back next year to see what she can do.

I had to feel sorry for Mr. Hudson. I am really fond of him. He tries so hard to make everyone happy. He said that he had read our preference sheets, and he knew what all of us had written on them.

"I won't stand in your way, and I hope you get just what you want, but make your plans to come back to Glenview. Glenview wants you. If you find out you won't be back, let me know as soon as possible, please. Don't wait until August to call from California to say you won't be back. Give me a chance. I know I can't get anyone as good as you, but let me try to get someone who is almost as good."

As usual, the entire faculty left the meeting laughing—not *at* him but *with* him, because his serious comments had been made in his usual jolly manner.

March 27

        Sanitation habits, personal cleanliness in particular, is a real problem with some of the students. And, of course, that goes back to the home and community. Body odor is the biggest bother. I had thought that with my bird-dog nose I wouldn't be able to stand the odor, but so far I haven't had any major problems.

The janitorial staff does a fine job; it's the eating problem that creates the mess at Glenview. The room cleanliness has greatly improved, however. Rarely a day goes by without someone commenting about what a pretty room we have. Just today, Travis said, "Miss Moran can't say that her room's the prettiest anymore."

Today we changed the three bulletin boards in the room. Some of the things that we used I've saved for years, but some of the things I made last summer in workshop. (Little did I realize, when I was attending that workshop, that the things I made would be adorning Glenview walls this year.) I cut out the letters during the ride to and from school. Jim and Kurt did the drawings that were needed.

I feel guilty about not allowing the students to do all of the work. I've always believed in student work, and these children could do more than just put up bulletin boards. Many draw well, and not only would they enjoy doing the boards, but they would learn a lot. But since time is so limited, I must put first things first. And first things here in my room must be reading, spelling, and history.

I've always used bulletin boards for adornment, class participation, creative expression, messages, etc., but I had never fully realized before that the bulletin board could be such a tremendous learning tool. These children take in every word. I'm glad they appreciate these things. I guess it's worth it all.

March 28

It makes a problem taking things to school. I get my share of deserved teasing. Molly won't let me forget that I wasn't going to take a thing to Glenview and Joe reminds me of all my broad statements every time I make a new bulletin board. In this case, it's nice to have been wrong and changed my mind. I never dreamed that the children would be so responsive. If they weren't I wouldn't wag things back and forth every day. I am afraid to take too many things for fear they will be destroyed, so I just take enough for the week ahead. My carpool co-worker always says, "I admire you for doing for them. They don't know how lucky they are to have someone who will put out so much effort." Her approving words always come at the right time.

I wouldn't tell any of the teachers how many hours it has taken to find interesting materials to fit the students' needs and exercises they can do. It would have been much easier to have tried to fill the gaps in a year or more. Randy gave me a set of the *Golden Book Encyclopedia* to use. I have gone through all my remedial reading material and pulled out every lesson that combines American history and reading skills. Marian found some good puzzles at the store, and I already had a book of history puzzles. I've just stopped trying to use the regular texts, except for certain parts; these children are simply not prepared for them.

Since the educational philosophy of this parish has always been that we are teaching children, not books, I don't have to worry about "covering the entire book." It's much easier to be able to suit the work to the children with the support of the Glenview administration as well as the central office, even if we never complete the books.

There's one thing for sure. You never know when you'll use something you learn. When I took that remedial reading course several years ago, the class concentrated on taking textbook materials and adapting them to various levels of learning. Every test, study guide, etc., that we made during that course had to be made for three levels of ability. I'm certainly getting plenty of practice now.

I couldn't do it, though, without Mrs. Lee, our wonderful teacher's aide. I was delighted when she was assigned to Glenview. She has already learned how to interpret all my handwritten work, complete with its insertions, notes, etc. After becoming so spoiled with the services of marvelous teachers' aides at Timberlane, I don't know if I could have made it without that help. Teachers' aides are the best addition to the school system since copying machines were invented.

These children at Glenview get their own help, too. The Negroes don't ask the teacher for help, though. They get it from one another constantly; they expect to do so. Some seem to have partners who have been helping them over reading and arithmetic hurdles for years. This may be one reason they don't work independently as well as the whites do.

The majority of the whites can read independently; that's one reason they don't depend on one another for help. The good Negro readers help the poor ones. These children love to hear one another read! A class of white children would be climbing the walls if a whole chapter of history were read to them, but the Negroes seem perfectly content. The white children could not stand for a class to move that slowly.

How different these classes are! What a challenge

these children present! How rewarding when I see I am
making progress!

March 30

The cookie problem—everybody
eating cookies in the classrooms, halls, etc.—got to the
point that the principal asked the faculty to check on the
matter. Today it turned out that a high-school girl was
selling them for her church, and the principal ordered
the sales stopped. He commented that he has had this
problem before. My first-period class still contains a few
"eaters," but my fourth- and fifth-period groups have
stopped.

Denise's information about her favorite teacher in
another school made me wonder about who else contributed to the problem.

Mrs. Luttrell was one of the nicest teachers I ever
had. When some kind of holiday came we always had a
party. Mrs. Luttrell let us sell candy, ice cream cones,
Cokes, and popcorn. We had fun going off the campus to
the store. When we got back to school we went around
taking orders.

Last week I faced a problem. My mother had under-
gone an operation at the Houston Medical Center, and I
had to be absent to be with her. I knew that a few days
with a substitute might make my classes regress, and I
certainly didn't want that! Therefore, I prepared the class
as well as I could and left the substitute many times the
amount of work I thought that the students could do. I
had a reason: Busy students are usually not discipline
problems.

When I returned today, I was greeted by a very sympathetic group who had only one complaint: "You left too much lessons." The excellent substitute, a young Negro recently graduated from college, had kept their feet to the fire. I was delighted!

The teachers were honored while I was gone—Teacher Appreciation Week. One day, each got an apple, and another day, coffee and doughnuts were served in the lounge—all compliments of the Glenview Student Council.

Charles has his version of school appreciation:

I hate to come to school, but I come anyway. I know that while I have a chance to come, I should come. One thing that I really hate is lesson. Lesson! lesson, that's all we do. We hardly ever have time to rest. One more thing that happens at school is they steal too much. After they steal, they could lie quick as 1, 2, 3.

April

April 2

Since the day I wore a bright yellow kettle-cloth dress with an embroidered border, my clothes have been a constant source of admiration. That day when Susie commented that my dress was beautiful, I simply said, "Thanks. I made it." I've never heard so many oohs and ahs! Now seldom does a day pass that I am not asked, "Did you make that dress, too?" I'm puzzled about their reactions. Maybe this makes them "identify" with me since many of their clothes are homemade. It almost makes me wish I were teaching them sewing.

But I guess I'll have to hem my dresses a little shorter. One of my students keeps telling me she thinks I look like a "grandma" because my dresses are too long. I wonder if she thinks I should wear mini-skirts. The Negro students don't wear their minis as short as the white girls do.

My fashionable student will have to get accustomed to my "grandma" dresses, and I'll have to get used to a clothing habit I'd never seen before: students wear jackets and coats all day long, no matter how warm it gets. I asked one of the Negro teachers why this was so, and she said they were afraid they would get stolen if they weren't on their backs.

It has been hard, indeed, to get used to the language

used casually by students and faculty alike at Glenview. This language would be unthinkable in polite society. Conversations can be peppered with "butt" and "ass," and I have even overheard a Negro teacher giving orders to students: "Get your tails back in those seats. You heard me; get your tails back in those seats!" I thought I must have been hearing things.

When some students passed outside our classroom window and one said to another, "I'll hit you in the ass," not a head in my classroom was raised in astonishment or even in recognition that something unusual had been said.

One student told one of the white transferees at another Negro school that if she didn't let her go to the bathroom, she would urinate on the floor. A boy, who had been refused permission to go to the restroom, said that he would bring a bucket to class with him. The teacher sent him to the principal's office. He soon returned to class, saying that the assistant principal had told him that he could keep the bucket in the principal's office. This was, of course, totally untrue, as verified by the teacher later. The thing that was so disturbing to my shocked friend was that this kind of conversation could evolve in a classroom and that the conversation was shared by the entire class. In our white culture only the crudest person would refer to a personal matter in mixed company.

In the lounge I have heard birth control discussed among adults completely without reticence. Maybe I'm old-fashioned, but discussions of this type in mixed groups still seem improper to me.

Home remedies were a topic in the lounge among some Negro faculty members today. Someone described medicine made from cobwebs, and one Negro man told of a remedy made from "cow shit." If these stories had been told in jest, I would have simply regarded the language as a sign of the times.

I really must be a "grandma!"

April 3

During a creative writing unit, the students are writing autobiographies. Their list of one hundred suggested titles includes a wide range of topics; therefore, I was surprised when this title was selected. Tonight I checked Elaine's paragraph entitled, "My Family Tree."

> My family doesn't have a tree to be called a family tree. If they did, I don't know about it. But if they do have one, they ought to at least let me know about it. If they don't have one in the family, I'm planning to put one in the family.

She knows the fundamentals of writing a paragraph; her limited experiences just don't include any knowledge of genealogy. I'm just now beginning to understand what the term "culturally deprived" really means.

Ronald also chose "My Family Tree."

> I had a tree. It was a family tree. It belonged to the whole family. We had it a long time. It was an old tree and we liked the tree. We cut the tree down because they were going to build a house and everybody hated it. My great grandmother left it for me.

I ponder these questions: How many of these students were read to as babes? How many ever shared a newspaper or magazine with their parents? How many ever took a family trip to view historic sites? It is hard to visualize a group that has such a limited experience for learning. The simple things that we take for granted have never been a part of their experiences. My heart bleeds for them.

They will have to gain many of their experiences vicariously, so maybe Joan's *Hi-Lights* will help some. How they love those magazines! I'm hoping our reading program is raising their vocabulary levels, too, as their vocabularies are so limited.

Now educators really have a problem to solve. The crux of this dilemma may resolve itself around the order of precedence of two important factors—cultural enrichment and "book learning."

Funds for enrichment—cultural and scholastic—are being provided by the federal government for Glenview, since poverty in the area qualifies it as a Title I school. These funds are based on student enrollment. The students may not attend regularly, but if the students live within the district they belong on the school roll in order for the system to be eligible for the funds. Parish and state funds are also provided on the same basis.

Now that the puzzle about class rolls is a little clearer, something else is puzzling me. Rumors again. Rumors are that a special faculty meeting is to be called to hear the complaints of students. The students don't like the way the white teachers are treating them—so the tales go. The rumors are flying about the nature of the complaints. I wonder if any of my students are complaining. Time will tell, I suppose.

One of my transferee friends is not complaining today. She has learned that her NDEA (National Defense Education Act) college loan balance is being reduced because she is working at Glenview. Every little bit helps.

April 5

The Sunday paper is full of the latest protesting. Parents are protesting to the school board about the lack of "quality" education, and the school board has worked out some plans for improving the system.

I can understand how the Negro teachers are having a difficult time making the adjustments necessary to teach in the white schools. The two systems are just different, and these differences call for many adjustments.

The Negro teachers in the segregated Negro schools did not have to plan as much work on as high a level as the white teachers have had to do to keep up with their students. White teachers have paced their classes much faster than was possible in the Negro schools.

As a general rule, the Negro children are not accustomed to doing homework. I had been warned that I could expect a very few—the exceptional—to complete homework consistently. This works in reverse in the white schools since only a few do not complete homework. There is a practical basis for this difference I'm sure. Crowded homes, lack of facilities or interest, lack of understanding and encouragement by parents because of educational background, and necessary home chores— all these things contribute to this. Not once since I have been here have I had a child ask for homework for an absentee or ask for missed work. In white schools conscientious parents go to great lengths to see that their children don't "get behind"; therefore, there are many requests for missed work. Often a student who anticipates being out requests work in advance. Naturally, classwork is planned differently when homework is anticipated.

Reference work assignments indicate a significant difference found by the two groups of teachers. White children begin reference homework in the elementary grades, and by the time they have reached high school, they are old hands at the job. The Negroes can certainly use reference materials well, but I can never make a reference homework assignment. Very few, if any, of my students have encyclopedias, although all eighty-eight have at least one or more television sets.

"Quality" education covers phases other than classwork and homework. Discipline is a big issue. It stands to reason that a person who spends a great deal of time handling discipline problems is going to have that much less time to work. Some of the Negro teachers who have mixed classes are having their share of problems. Lack of parental support from an extremely small group of whites contributes to this problem. The Negro teachers aren't the only ones having problems, however. Some white teachers naturally took their problems with them when they transferred; if they couldn't control a class of white children, it is too much to expect them to control a class of Negro children.

Then, too, many Negro teachers now in white schools use variations in pronouncing words understandable to the Negroes but not to the white children. The Negro dialect and colloquial expressions cause problems of communication similar to those encountered when a Bostonian and a Cajun attempt to communicate.

The school board has devised some promising innovations. Experienced teachers, called coordinating teachers, will work with individual teachers to see that the program is carried on uniformly. All teachers will be evaluated, and those who are not doing their jobs successfully will be dismissed even if they are on tenure. The non-graded elementary school and the phasing of junior-high and high-school students into classes on their working levels will be used to meet their needs, interests, and abilities. New guidelines will be established for discipline and attendance requirements.

This educational world is going through some significant changes. Many of these things, such as dismissing teachers for incompetency, should have come years ago. It is a shame that it took a court order to bring about these far-reaching changes.

Many are eagerly awaiting the results of a test case in which the superintendent has asked the school board to dismiss a Negro teacher who is said to be incompetent.

The Sunday paper has much food for thought today. The current problems of education in Newton Parish certainly received good coverage. Since the problems have been brought out in the open, this should cut out some of the undertone in the community.

April 6

Sure enough. The faculty meeting was held today. Mr. Hudson had the entire faculty together at first; then he dismissed all of the Negroes.

Mr. Hudson sat down in front of us "to talk things over," he said. He began by saying that he had been getting reports. "The smartest students feel dumb. They think that the teachers are repeating what they already know. These students are like most other students; they're grade conscious. Get to know them. Read their cumulative records to find the reasons the children are the way they are. Many are from big families with no fathers. They live in homes with a hand-to-mouth existence that doesn't produce an atmosphere for learning. About ninety percent of the Glenview enrollment attend classes; five percent don't want to be there. These students are adjusting to their new teachers better than I thought they would by this time. In fact, we're about ten days ahead of schedule according to my thinking."

The complaints weren't nearly as bad as we had imagined!

April 7

Southern Association evaluation—of all things to do now. At least we aren't going to have to go through the evaluation procedure with visitors, etc., to get the school accredited. The visitation of the committee has been postponed until next year. We have been assigned to committees, though. This means that we must help accumulate the information for the fall visit. I am wondering how we can judge the school fairly. How can we, as total strangers to their way of life, present an accurate picture of their community? When I think about that first year at Timberlane—how many hours we spent and how conscientiously we worked—I wonder how this will come out.

Why are these Negro schools so different? A friend discussed this with a Negro teacher who said, "Almost all

Negro teachers teach exactly the way they were taught themselves. They pace their classes the same way, and they are accustomed to the noise, absenteeism, tardiness, movement, and eating. This is all they have ever known. It will take years to change these ways."

"Middle-class American standards can't be shoved on these people overnight," has been said many times.

"Basically the difference is cultural," my little friend from Clinton told me. "I wish the crossover workshop had centered around cultural differences. These differences are what I didn't know when I started, and I didn't know that I didn't know the differences between the two cultures."

Was this cultural? I saw a young white teacher fold up today. When she walked into her room, she found written in huge letters on the chalkboard: "Mrs. Pittman is a whore." She cried and cried. She is young and took it personally. I don't think I would have. It probably consoled her some when she heard that this had already happened in another school to a young, attractive white teacher. There will be this kind of thing for a while yet.

Today when we were walking to the lounge, we heard some students call, "The honkies are coming! The honkies are coming!" I had almost forgot the warning about "honkies." Come to think of it, I haven't seen it written anywhere at Glenview.

April 8

These students and their lack of supplies bug me. Now it is the pencil problem. They rarely come to class with pencils and paper. They simply assume that they can go by the office and get a pencil.

I explained to my class today that a student should keep one pencil for at least a week or two. Mike explained his position: "I get one at the office every day. That tells you I am trying, and I'm too poor to buy one."

I checked with the office force about the school policy. Apparently, they weren't aware of the fact that the same students were there for a handout everyday.

"I don't think that this is developing desirable habits in the students," I told them. "They are not learning to care for materials or to appreciate the gift. They just expect another handout when the need arises."

"We'll stop handing out pencils," I was told. It hurts to see tax money spent to inculcate a bad habit!

April 9

It happened today!

Many transferees met with the "top brass" of the central office to get first-hand information about the assignment of teachers for next year. The rumors had been making the rounds again, so the teachers asked to hear the plan "from the horse's mouth."

When the Lamar teachers arrived, they were upset about a riot at their school today. Their feelings and those of other hostile teachers generated dissatisfaction throughout the crowd. Of course, everyone wanted to hear about the "bad grades" protest against a white teacher at Lamar. In turn, the superintendent wasn't very happy; therefore, the group was not what would be described as congenial.

The transferees did get the information they were

seeking: Anyone with fifteen or more years of teaching can expect to be returned to his former position. Those with about ten years will be returned the next year, and the third year, all the others should return. Also, almost all first- and fourth-year teachers can expect to be sent to the opposite race's schools.

Mr. Wheat listened to the barrage of painful questions, and then made a significant statement. "None of us is guiltless. The Negroes were denied an education before 1967, and we are at fault because we allowed the state to support two systems." He finally said—wearily, I thought—"It is to our advantage to get you back where you will bellyache less."

One teacher wanted to know why white teachers had been sent to Negro schools and "forgotten"—that is, the school board supervisors and administrators were nowhere in sight. "Let's face it," Mr. Wheat answered. "Most of the school board members are not interested in visiting schools, and due to lack of money, there aren't enough supervisors to get around to all the schools."

From the comments after the meeting, I concluded that many were still disgruntled and felt that their questions were not answered to their satisfaction.

During my thirty-minute ride home, I was alone with my thoughts about the baffling school situation that had aroused so many questions from the transferees and general public as well.

I thought if there were any philosophy involved it was to leave the Negro to handle the school as he wished. After all, it was a segregated school existing in a subculture with entirely different folkways and mores.

The lack of understanding between those in authority of each other's culture was enough to stymie those who would have liked things done differently. Until now Negroes operated their schools according to their standards in a way they interpreted the job. True, they attended the same parish meetings, filled out identical forms, etc. The school board always allowed for differences among schools, and Negro schools were just another type of difference. The Negro subculture was different, the students in the two systems were different, and, therefore, the two programs were different.

As for the school board members, they are paid for monthly meetings (not very much, though), but who could pay them for the day and night meetings constantly held during the period between the court order and the final assignment of teachers? When would they visit the schools? After all, they have full-time jobs, too.

Why didn't the Negro schools have supplies? Superintendent Wheat said earlier that he didn't know what became of the supplies. A school board member has asked for an investigation of the matter to find out what happened. I don't believe that the F.B.I. could come up with an exact answer, but the frequent "break-ins" must be one big factor. The students don't trust each other and the teachers don't trust the students. There must be much petty thievery for this distrust to be so prevalent.

What about the noise? One Negro supervisor said that it is the result of their culture. Perhaps so, but I suspect it is simply the lack of training involved in learning to be quiet and observe routine discipline in a school. The "muttering" is just another way to rebel, I think. I wonder if it goes back to slave days. Have the Negroes been forced into such narrow lives with such few free choices that they reject any discipline at all when left to themselves? Did discipline in years past become associated with the orders of masters? In any case, this is a new world, 1970, and integration must involve some sloughing off of cultural patterns not compatible in an integrated society.

The astonishing thing, when I look back over the time at Glenview and my years of teaching elsewhere, is that it all seems so different from that other world—the white world in which I have lived. I have found out that the Negro has, in reality, lived in his own world, a sub-culture so completely hidden that the average white man didn't really know it existed. All we knew was what was on the surface for white people to see. The state and parish provided them with magnificent modern buildings, exactly as they did the white schools, issued ample supplies and textbooks based on their orders, and hired certified teachers and principals. It all looked good—until the transferees looked behind the curtain and discovered a totally different picture.

April 10

Another first—a Negro teacher had a fight with her husband when he came to get her after school yesterday. She obviously didn't want to go with him. She kicked and fought, and he fought back. The screaming and the commotion aroused the attention of many teachers and students. Would white teachers do this?

One of the main causes for verbal attacks among the

students is "talking about my mother." A weapon frequently used to "get back" is an accusation about the father, such as, "Your daddy doesn't shave," or "Your daddy drives a Model-T."

One day when I heard this last statement being used in anger, I couldn't resist saying, "My son would love a Model-T." Both belligerents stopped fussing and looked at me as if I'd lost my marbles.

I was amazed at Stan's honesty when he wrote about solving the TV problem in his home:

> We solved the television problem by arguing, fighting, kicking, scarthing, tuning, changing channels, questing, begging and crying.

Who can identify with him? On the other hand, Rosalie wrote her essay on "Good Children":

> Good children do not fight, and do not write on the school wall, and do not cut class. And they will not talk back to the teacher when she say something to them. And not talk about their teachers. And when the teacher tell them to do something they will do it. And when the teacher tell them to work they will do just what she told them to do. And they will respect grown people.

April 13

I have worked on nothing so hard as getting the students to improve their language. I have noticed Grace admonishing her classmates, "Quit using old folks' talk!"

I decided to capitalize on this expression to make a bulletin board. (I observed earlier that they use bulletin boards the way they were intended to be used; they read everything on them.) Kurt made me some pretty letters spelling out "Old Folks' Talk," and I put a "wash" of blue and red on a big piece of brown paper. I wrote the incorrect forms of words, crossed them out in red, and then wrote the correct forms under them. It took us hours to make it, but we were pleased with the results.

After we finished it, Jim went to his sister's house, and when he told her what we had done, she was a bit worried. Wouldn't this antagonize the students? Would they consider this mockery? When Jim told me about her reaction, I became worried, too. I hadn't thought about it from that angle.

I decided to put the board up anyway. Needless to say, I was dying to get the reaction of the students.

When the students saw the new bulletin board, they immediately crowded around to read it. Dora and Betsy started telling me what "old folks' " words I had left out.

I wanted to see what the juniors would say when they came for their class, which meets in my room during my free period. Their response was the same: Mrs. Culbertson, you left out this and that. One sure thing—they enjoyed it immensely.

All week they enjoyed that board. They invited their friends in to look over the list. Dora and Betsy got together and made me a list of all the words and expressions I had left out so I could make another bulletin board.

When I told a supervisor about my experience with the bulletin board, she sent me a list that had been compiled in the central office. The list contained very few words that we hadn't used. The obvious ones started the list.

April 15

A white counselor in a Negro school had an interesting case. A very intelligent student, a boy, went to her to discuss his problem—he hated whites. And he went on to reveal why this feeling had reached such disturbing proportions. His daddy owns a handy-man shop. The boy wanted to transfer to a formerly all-white school, when there was the opportunity to do so under freedom-of-choice. His dad refused to allow it because "the white folks won't like it." (And Dad had his side; he was afraid of wrecking their financial security with whites taking their business away from him, or banks not lending him money, or any number of possible reprisals.) The boy wanted to wear an Afro haircut, but Dad gave the same reason. It seemed to the boy that whites always stood in the way of the things he wanted to do. "Everytime I wanted to do something, my daddy was concerned with whether or not the whites would like it."

April 16

Poor sewing teacher—she was actually crying today over the new steam iron stolen from her room. She was ill and had a substitute Friday, and the substitute didn't lock the closet in the home-ec department. (Teaching sewing without an iron is next to impossible.) And she had worked so hard to get that iron, too!

She got the iron when she exchanged an unused, not-needed dress form provided by the school board. The sales lady at the local store where the exchange was made commented, "I don't know what is needed for equipment

in home-ec, but I know I replaced a stainless steel set of
pots and pans last year. How did they wear out?" (Seem-
ingly they didn't wear out; they disappeared.) I never
did miss any pots or pans when I taught home-ec, but I
missed paring knives and measuring spoons. The department couldn't keep those items.

She has really had her problems teaching sewing.
There is material provided by federal funds to distribute.
This is frustrating because it is so time-consuming. Then
she has to issue needles (some Negro schools issue needles
every hour), bobbins, scissors, etc. Having taught in
white schools in which the girls provide their own materials and have to keep up with them themselves, the frustrated teacher says that she will have to get out of home
economics if she continues teaching in a Negro school.
The situation is just too much to endure.

For the first few weeks she was here, so few students
had material to work with that she got desperate and
wrote notes home to the parents explaining the students'
needs. Almost all managed to get what was needed.

When things like this come up, I'm glad I don't have
to keep up with all that equipment. That's one reason I
got out of that field, anyway.

April 17

It may have been just talk, but I was
shocked! One of the Negro men teachers was talking in
the lounge to a group at sixth period. "There's a big
problem every spring at Glenview," he said. "The boys
think they prove their manhood by the number of babies

they father. They go around boasting to each other, 'I'm going to put a baby in her.' " The babies conceived in the spring arrive during football season, so they've acquired a name—"football babies." The girls miss the first semester and then return the last half.

It would seem incredible except one upset Negro lad lamented to his white teacher only yesterday, certainly in a different vein, "I'm in bad trouble. I'm so worried. I done got me a family, I'm going to have to settle down and I'm not ready."

"When are you going to get married?" the teacher asked.

"I'm going to wait until I have a good job."

In contrast to the worried father, this one was extremely happy. There was a shocked white secretary at one school when a senior Negro boy excitedly shared the news, "I'm the father of twins!"

"Oh, I didn't know that you were married."

"I'm not, but I'm planning to get married this summer."

Then there's the business that frequently turns up in the senior-high classes, with a student asking to be excused from classes to take care of her ill child, or to do some necessary shopping for her child, and the like.

Does this "baby problem" have any connection with Paul's second wish? In my years of teaching, I've never had a white twelve-year-old *boy* mention such a wish:

> If I had three wishes I would wish that I had a pony to ride. My second wish I would wish to be a lover. My third wish for money and a good place to stay.

April 20

All day yesterday and part of the day today, a seminar on Americanism versus Communism was held for the juniors and seniors. The teachers gave rave notices to the student speakers. Mr. Hudson was so pleased that he called a special faculty meeting to let the other teachers hear the student essays. That was an impressive program! Mr. Hudson beamed when the faculty rated the speeches so highly. (They were excellent.) Then he added a humorous touch with a serious undertone: "There are some fence jumpers and 'woods' boys in that bunch, too."

April 21

Even the old business of writing lines for punishment takes a different twist at Glenview. When I picked up these lines from a child who had decided to get his done during my class, I was startled. A white child assigned lines like this would provoke the parents into taking action against the teachers, principal, school board, and everybody else they could think of who might be involved. Some teacher had assigned: "I will not act a fool when you absent."

Speaking of court action reminds me that the school board was successful in dismissing the incompetent teacher who had tenure. Things are looking up! This could pave the way for the dismissal of other deadheads.

April 22

The P.T.A. meeting tonight created quite a dilemma for me. The story around school was that the Negro teachers don't attend P.T.A. meetings, and most white transferees had orders from their husbands that they were not going into the Glenview neighborhood at night. I hated to let the principal down, but I couldn't go by myself. Mr. Hudson had assured us that there was no need to worry. I finally made up my mind to go when Jim said that he'd go, too.

It turned out to be a "blast," as the students say. Strangely enough, the faculty in attendance was predominantly white. The speaker was a "sixty-five-years-young" Negro woman. As district president of the P.T.A. Council, she works with adults and has developed an unusual ability to communicate with them. Her honors include an invitation by President Eisenhower to serve on a committee for race relations. She was one of the liveliest and most humorous speakers I have ever heard, and her timing was perfect. She also had the ability to say very personal things without trespassing.

"A disturbed child cannot learn," she explained. "If you and the 'old man' have a knock-down, drag-out fight before the kids leave for school, the kids are going to go to school disturbed," she continued. "I know he's got it coming, but wait 'til the children are off to school; then take him out in the back yard and 'let him have it.' "

She continued, "Some teen-agers asked me if I believed the story they'd been hearing about God being dead. I told those children that I didn't know, but judging from my experiences with Him, I'll take Him dead or alive." She displayed an unusual ability to transmit a serious thought while at the same time filling the auditorium with laughter.

At one point in her speech, she explained that a

hungry child can't learn. "Almost any mother can afford to feed her children breakfast before sending them off to school, and if any of you can't afford lunch for them, all you have to do to get them free lunch is come up here to the school and sign a piece of paper . . . if you're not too lazy." Then, very humorously, she added, "Of course, I'm not talking about y'all here tonight, but I'm talking about those who didn't make it here, so y'all be sure to tell them to come on up here and sign for free lunches if they aren't too lazy." She commented that where she worked, she had seen a couple come up and sign for free lunches for their children, and then she watched them as they drove off in their Cadillac.

"You may not be able to provide your children with the things they need if you don't do without some things yourself. When I was raising my children, picture-shows were five cents. Five cents would also buy a pair of socks, and that's what my children needed. I didn't go to a show for many years because I knew I needed to spend the money on the needs of my children. That's what you folks are going to have to do to raise your standards at home. The school and churches can't do much until you do your part."

She got her message across!

After the P.T.A. meeting, the parents visited the classrooms. It was an exact duplication of the type of program that we had had on such occasions in other schools in which I have taught. About twelve parents came by. I discussed their children and their problems in exactly the same way I had done with white parents at other schools, and their responses were the same:

"He can do better work, but he plays too much. I have to persuade him to work."

"That is the problem we've had since he started school."

"Robert is late almost every morning. He misses the beginning of the class."

"He won't be late anymore. I send him to school at 7:00 o'clock when I go to work. He is just staying out on the grounds and playing ball too long."

"That spelling list you gave Doretha has really reviewed me. I haven't had some of those words for years. We are enjoying doing spelling together."

"I appreciate all the lovely charts Larry has drawn for the class. He is certainly a talented boy."

"He loves to draw. He could draw all the time. I am glad he can do it for the class."

Another pleasant surprise! I'm still shaking my head in amazement about that super P.T.A. meeting. The choir was great, the speaker couldn't have been better, the parents were very appreciative, and the refreshments made a good ending. Mr. Hudson was right. There was nothing to worry about.

April 23

I have found the magic words: "You want a good education." Any time the students slack off in their work, all I need to do is remind them of this idea: "You want a good education, don't you?", and they get back to work in a hurry. Poor, poor children! They want a good education, but they have no idea what they are going to have to do to get one. Maybe many would get discouraged too soon. They have no way of knowing that their irregular attendance, poor study habits, lack of supplies, and lack of punctuality affects their efforts to get an education.

These comments about an education show how some feel:

"I want an education to be popular."

"I want an education because I want to have a chance in life to be something and to be somebody instead of an uneducated person who don't have a chance to get a good education. I want a good education because I want a good job and I don't want to work in a house for anyone because I would feel like a prisoner in jail."

"I want to be proud of myself and for others to think that way."

"I want a good education because I don't want to pitch pennies."

"I want an education because life isn't very sweet without it. Without an education you might as well be dead."

"I want an education because I want to be grow up to be somebody."

"I want an education because I can't get a job without one."

Mr. Hudson realizes the education situation, though. He told us at a faculty meeting that all teachers are going to heaven. "Keep those children in those rooms and teach them. It is a sin not to teach," he added. "Education," he said, "is like football. The play might hit them differently this time."

I know that Mr. Hudson gets called "Uncle Tom" (his name happens to be Tom), and I've thought about that a lot. I believe it is just an easy way, really, for people to explain a phenomenon—a truly selfless man with feeling and concern for humanity. It's such a shock to find a Mr. Hudson when most people are strictly concerned with themselves—what they can get out of life every day. They couldn't care less about humanity, least of all about a bunch of underprivileged children who require superhuman effort sometimes. After all, Mr. Hudson makes a good salary and enjoys a high status. He could take it easier, as a lot of principals do. And his position especially stands out in a community where, unfortunately, almost everybody has such a low position. Some people might exploit the situation to exalt themselves. Not Thomas Hudson. So, if Uncle Tom means a very fine gentleman devoted to uplifting his people the hard way—training their children in spite of all the handicaps—then I go along with that.

And the name, I suppose, implies that he gets along with whites. He sees us just as he does the students—people with problems not of our own making. White teachers from another cultural background thrown into this environment are likely to experience traumatic feelings, and Mr. Hudson seemed to be aware of this from the very beginning. He has to understand the situation to have the patience and compassion with all of us that he has. And he has to have something special to keep this whole bunch from complaining. I haven't heard a single teacher, black or white, make one complaint about him. When you come to think of that, it's really something!

He certainly must be an Uncle Tom if there ever was one.

April 24
          One problem of white teachers working in an all-Negro school (and the problem probably has its counterpart in the reverse situation) is the matter of our friends and neighbors when we get home. In a sense, we are working in a different culture, and the home-folks don't share our experience. It is even difficult to find the proper words to try to communicate so as to avoid further misunderstandings between the groups. For instance, the persistent question of whether or not the Negro child can really learn takes many forms.

"Did any make 'A's'?" one dear old lady wanted to know this afternoon.

This was hard to answer satisfactorily because the general public conceives of standards for each school grade—not standards for each pupil. It was hard to explain that I had completely changed my work to fit their needs and abilities and then graded accordingly.

Mr. Wheat told us at the "crossover" meeting that some of the adjustment problems are being caused by teachers who are trying to stick to their old standards, mythical levels that some teachers think all children should reach. Standards have to be for individuals, and most people realize that, I think. Several of the transferees at Glenview have commented that they themselves didn't realize that they were so flexible, but they have changed their work for these children.

The first few weeks, one of the junior-high math

teachers was very frustrated trying to get the students to add fractions. Finally, in desperation, she invited her supervisor, an exceptionally capable Negro woman, to help her with her problem. The supervisor sat in on two classes and came to the conclusion that the work was too difficult for the majority of the students. The supervisor told the math teacher, "You will have to go back to fifth, fourth, maybe second grade to find work that they can do." The teacher then went back to the addition and subtraction of whole numbers. Every student was required to make an addition chart. Addition was not such a problem for them, but subtraction, where re-grouping was necessary, was completely foreign to almost all. After spending two weeks with subtraction, the teacher felt rewarded when a quiet little girl, with a look of surprise on her face, said, "I can work it!"

The transferees have tried to take these children where we found them and work out a program just for them. Most of the teachers agree with me that lack of time is a big handicap. I would love to have more time for them to practice reading. I keep reminding them that if they want to make a ball team, they practice, and that's what they need so desperately in reading—practice, practice, practice!

The first six weeks I made out my grades at home and then recorded them on permanent records at school. Oddly enough, I found very few who did not continue the same grade pattern. One boy made a "B" in history for me, and he had made "D's" the other six weeks. He was one of the best students I had, too, and one of the few who consistently completed his homework assignments. There were a few who dropped a grade, and a few who raised grades—perfectly routine.

April 27

I decided to boost Frederick's school work by telephoning his parents. He has kept us all laughing, but he hasn't produced the work he could. I asked him for his telephone number.

"My mother will be mad if you call her," he told me and said that he didn't remember his number.

I secured the number from the office. The mother spoke sensibly, saying she had had no trouble with his studying in elementary school, but he seemed to have stopped working when he got to junior high. (This is common for many twelve-year-olds.) She assured me that he would change back to his former habits. Now I am anxious to see what Frederick's reaction will be to our conversation.

I made another telephone call after I got home, and I'm eager to see the results. Betsy has a habit of constantly mumbling in a mocking fashion—not loud enough to be understood but loud enough to be disturbing. Nothing I have tried has stopped her from doing this. I knew she objected to "so much lessons," and I have taken the time more than once to discuss the situation with her. But she continues to disturb the class. I reported all this to her mother last night when I telephoned. When I finished, her mother said, "I don't know what she's been doing, but whatever she's been doing, she won't do it again!"

No one could ask for better cooperation than that!

April 28

Well, Frederick worked like an angel today, and he didn't pout—no mumbling from Betsy, either. What a change! I hope it lasts!

This was my first attempt to use old methods to prod students, and it certainly got results. I'll try some more.

The office had such a time finding the telephone numbers that I decided to check with Mrs. Jones, my predecessor, who is still at Glenview. After I told her what I planned to do, she said that she was not surprised at the numbers I needed. They were the same students who hadn't worked well for her.

I took this opportunity to tell Mrs. Jones how much I appreciated her, for she had turned over some good classes to me, which made my job much easier. She said, "You don't fool the students nor the teachers. They soon find out who means business. The children respect you when they know you are trying to help them."

This was the first time I felt genuine rapport with a Negro teacher. Mrs. Jones does a good job and has excellent discipline. I think that if I stay at Glenview, we can work together to train some good students.

April 29

We were seeing the moon-shot on film, and I was flabbergasted—not at the men walking on the moon, but at my seventh-grade students at Glenview.

"Do you believe he really stepped on the moon?" Floyd asked as we watched.

"Surely. You just saw him, didn't you?"

"*I don't believe it.* That's just make-believe."

I thought he was kidding until I realized that every last member of the class felt the same way. *It wasn't true; they didn't believe it*! Now what do I do?

May

May 1

Got a card today from my sister, Nancy, who teaches in Tulsa, Oklahoma. She said that at her school "black" is a taboo word. This brings to mind the many times that I have thought about the problems created by the lack of communication—not only between the whites and blacks, but also among the blacks themselves. For instance, at some of the Negro schools here, the transferee teachers were told to say "black," and yet here at Glenview I've noticed "black" and "nigger" used frequently by the Negroes as derogatory names. I am now accustomed to the students saying, "Mrs. Culbertson, make that nigger leave me alone," or "Black boy, you better get out of my way."

This suggests another bad word, "boy"—about the most insulting word one can use to address a male student at Glenview. The second day I was here, Myron said, "I found out that that new white teacher calls people 'boy'!" I didn't ask any questions, but the expression on his face told me that this was not a good word. I've tried hard to break the habit I've used with youngsters for years. After all, what do you call twelve- and thirteen-year-old boys? Maybe there are others who realize now what Myron asked me one day recently, " 'Boy' isn't always bad, is it?"

Then there's another problem that has come up

among the teachers about names—first names, that is. One of my friends was called aside and politely told that she should not call the young secretary or any other Negroes by their first names. At another school, one of my shocked friends couldn't believe it when she heard her first name being used.

If everyone took life as lightly as Frederick does, words wouldn't become problems. That Frederick! He was at it today. Mrs. Jones sent a very light-skinned girl on an errand to my room today. After she left, Frederick asked, "Is that your sister?"

"No, my niece."

"Do you expect us to believe that?" Albert asked.

"I don't know. Do you?"

It amused the group that I played Frederick's game. Every class needs a Frederick!

May 4

Learning ability. It is interesting to see how many people—both teachers and laymen—ask me that poignant question: *"Can they learn?"*

"Yes, of course, they can!"

The sad thing is the gaps in their education, the lack of so much we have taken for granted that all American children know. They *can* learn. I'm convinced by their performance, but they haven't learned as much as one would expect.

I have one student who must have a very high native intelligence. No I.Q. test would reflect it, I think. But it has to be there. He is far better than any other student in history, but he doesn't know the fundamentals of spelling and grammar. I can hardly read his writing, but his memory is fantastic. To help the class have a better understanding of the Civil War, I asked Carlton to do some extra work. He reviewed several chapters from *Our Free Nation*. I have never heard anything like it before. He actually remembered the material so well that the students could follow him in their books. And he didn't have the book or a single note with him!

I decided that Carlton must have stayed up all night to memorize that material, so today I assigned him a short chapter during the class period. I wanted to see. *He did the same thing in one reading.* This boy could be taught anything!

And Carlton is not by himself. I don't have any other such exceptional students (you wouldn't expect it in any class), but I do have many who can learn *what they are taught.*

Their cumulative records don't reflect it, however. The intelligence quotients of my students range from 50 to as high as 100. (The average person usually shows an intelligence quotient of 90-110). Carlton has an I.Q. of 95. I know that this is not correct, and I question the accuracy of the test scores. The test that has been in use in this parish is not valid for them, or there have been some serious errors in the administration of it. I rather suspect the former. It is a test that calls for average reading ability, and many of these children cannot read at grade level. These students aren't test-conscious anyway. There must be an instrument on the market that would properly evaluate these culturally deprived youngsters. We are asked to phase, or group, them for instruction, using test data as one criterion. But my judgment of classroom performance certainly doesn't agree with the test data!

The difficult parts-of-speech concept is one criterion

for my judgment that they can be taught. These children recognize parts of speech so well that I eliminated this phase of the English work immediately. There are so many more important things that they need to know anyway. They memorize well, but according to their math teachers, they lack reasoning ability.

So many factors affect learning, and no one has ever determined exactly the part that motivation plays. Most of these students have a strong motivator—"I'm going to get a good education so I can get a good job."

If only I could wave a magic wand . . . !

May 5

Sometimes I pinch myself to see if it is really true. I can't believe that now when I enter A5, my classroom, at 8:00 a.m. to find a group of big boys congregated talking that I just tease a little, and they get the message right away. "These seventh graders really grew overnight!" I'll say. They laugh as they hurriedly leave the room. Less than three months ago, these same big boys would have frightened me out of my wits!

Betsy has behaved beautifully since her mother gave her the word. I like that kind of result—no more mumbling. My phone calls have certainly paid off!

A jam session at home this afternoon proved to be very interesting. Kurt and his buddies were discussing the "students only" assembly held at Timberlane this morning. They said the meeting, which attempted to reach an understanding of Timberlane's problems, was quite confusing at times. In general, it turned out to be a "pat 'em on the back" or "peace" session. The uneasy calm was broken, however, when a black girl called attention to the fact that the chairman had referred to "white guys" and "black boys." "These are men, not boys," she said. This statement brought cheers and clenched fists from several black "men." She also asked that the Negroes who enrolled at Timberlane during the crossover be referred to simply as "students" not "new students" or "transferees." The calm returned but was broken again when a black student questioned a white girl's pronunciation of "Negro" and stated that he preferred "black" or "Afro-American." Through it all, the student-council president, who led the discussion, remained unruffled. The meeting left everyone a little confused but fairly certain that some good had been accomplished by airing the views of both races.

It's interesting to get a different slant to the black-white mixing problems.

May 6
    Improvement programs of several types are being planned for this summer.

A non-fee summer school program will be available for six weeks from 8:00 a.m. until 11:00 a.m. from June 1 through July 10. Since Glenview is in a Title I area, this program will be free to any who attend. All the students are asked to do is get to class everyday unless they are ill.

"If the Negroes would come to school regularly and take advantage of the regular school session, the taxpayers wouldn't need to provide another opportunity for them to miss," one of my irate neighbors said. There are many people who feel the same way. Then, too, the whites have to pay unless they attend Title I non-fee summer schools instead of the schools in the white areas, and I've never known a white student who attended the free program.

There is also to be an opportunity school for teachers, but this includes both races. The principals are recommending teachers who have had problems in classroom management, in understanding children, and in instructing children. The teacher must agree to spend four or five weeks this summer working with successful, experienced teachers who are instructing in the summer program. A school of this kind should help, because only the most capable teachers will be selected for models. This sounds great!

The Newton Parish School Board is also trying to do something about the speech problems of Negro teachers. There have been so many complaints that something *had* to be done. A summer program is planned, and all teachers are asked to have their speech checked. A white principal said that he went first to have his speech checked, hoping that all of his teachers would follow his example.

A friend told me that she was calling out spelling words to her little daughter. "Pronounce them just as a Negro does, Mama, so I can understand Mrs. Lyttle tomorrow," the child requested of her.

I have to laugh about this. I remember my painful days in a college speech class when a New Englander tried to get me to "pronounce words right."

May 7

$$$ Doctor bills $$$
Sue has been having severe headaches for days. She

went to the doctor today, and he had a surprising bit of advice. "It is strictly your nerves," he told her. "And you are not by yourself. You would not believe the number of black and white teachers I am treating for nerves. You must learn to ignore much that you see. Do what you can to help, but, remember, you cannot perform miracles."

He gave her some pills to help her relax.

Sue said that the one thing that has helped her to live through the "crossover" has been the realization that black teachers and white teachers in similar situations are all having the same struggle. She's consoled, too, by the fact that she hasn't had a hospital visit for ulcers as some blacks and whites have.

Some of the Negro teachers haven't made it. One Negro called to tell his white principal that he had simply had all he could take. A little seventh-grade white girl had given him so much trouble that day that he decided he absolutely couldn't stand any more. Another Negro cross-over teacher told her white co-workers that she wanted to get back to black students because she related better to them.

Some teachers—black and white—are using their sabbatical leaves as a way out of the situation. They would rather go back to studies than stay with this. Before the crossover, I had enough illnesses for the rest of my lifetime. I'm thankful that I am free of nausea, headaches, and sleeplessness, at last!

May 8   The lack of background among
these poor Negro children is almost incomprehensible.

Cambodia? Cambodia?

An American history teacher in a black high school wanted to locate Cambodia today after Nixon's talk about the invasion. He asked the class where it was. "Where is Cambodia?" he repeated. Still no one answered. There was a long silence. "Surely, someone knows where Cambodia is."

Finally a low voice in the classroom was heard to say, "I think she be absent today."

It is not too surprising that he thought Cambodia was a person's name. The names of some Negro students are certainly different from my former students. There is Tremendous Stewart, and there are youngsters named Celestial, Okra, Corn, No No, Taimosis, Haile Selassie, and Unice, to cite a few—to say nothing of Female (pronounced "feemollie"), Love, and Office. Certainly adds variety!

Schools are as bad as the navy or army for rumors. Rumors! Rumors! Rumors! The rumor now making the rounds is that school will be dismissed one week early because of the *rumors* about riots, vandalism, gang fights, etc., which are to occur (so rumor has it) on the last day of school. Of course, the students are not supposed to have this bit of information. Suddenly, one day soon, the teachers will say to the students, "So long. See you next year!" It is very dramatic, but I don't believe it will happen that way.

May 11

I've made an appalling discovery. A white physical education teacher told the lounge group that students in some of her classes eat clay. She said that some of the girl students interrupted a ball game, crawled across a fence, and before her eyes, started eating clay. Some of us could hardly believe it.

Later today another teacher, who had been shocked by the story, asked her senior girls, "Is it true that some people eat clay?"

"Yes 'um, it is so. We love it."

"How many of you have eaten clay?" she asked.

All answered in the affirmative.

"How does it taste?" the teacher continued.

One girl asked her, "Do you know in the spring how good it smells when it rains? Clay tastes just that good."

The students freely talked about eating clay and added some more pointers.

"The best is by the pond."

"I like mine best cooked with water," someone said.

"I bake mine," another commented.

"Pregnant women especially like it."

I'll take their word for it that it is good; I don't plan to try it.

May 12

Mental telepathy? *The Daily Citizen* could not have overheard the clay discussion in the lounge yesterday, but this morning's paper contains an article about it. It says that minerals are lacking in the diet if clay or starch is eaten. I wonder if these students eat starch, too. That may be the reason that paste was a favorite food of some of my elementary school classmates.

Glenview had its first style show today. It was quite

an experience for the teacher and the students. The girls were bubbling with joy. The complimentary reports made me wish that I could have attended.

I meant to check to see if all the garments were finished on time. That sewing teacher means what she says, and she said that they were going to participate—even if they had to hold the unfinished garment up for the audience to see. I believe that I would have heard about it if this had actually happened. I did hear that the teacher was exhausted from prodding.

I recall how slowly my students worked when I first came. What I had planned for them to do in twenty minutes took an hour. I kept pacing them a little faster and a little faster until now they are working almost as fast as the classes I left. I might have been wrong to do this. They just don't seem to be in the mad rush that most of us whites are, but I couldn't resist teaching them some organization to save time and energy. By having other work ready for them to do as soon as they complete one assignment, there's no time left for a recess. They also don't have to wait for the slower ones and can pace themselves so that they can get the "extras."

Anyway, I've found out that it is habit as much as anything else that makes some work so slowly!

May 13

The Annual Choir Concert was tonight. Some of the white teachers have been surprised that the Negroes still sing Negro spirituals. We're glad they still appreciate one of their greatest musical contributions. And they sing them well! I didn't get to hear

them sing this time, but I did hear the beautiful singing
at the P.T.A. meeting.

May 14
       Another problem appeared today,
just when I thought I had stumbled on almost all of them.

"We won't be here tomorrow; so don't give that
test."

"What do you mean, you won't be here tomorrow?"

"Cleveland is having field day, and we are going
visiting."

When I asked one of the Negro teachers about this,
she said, "There won't be a handful of seventh graders
here tomorrow. All of them will go to field day at Cleveland. That's the best day of the year, and most of them
like to go back to their old school."

Wonder how many students will come tomorrow . . .?

Strange things happened among some of the high-
school students today, too.

The seniors are getting ready for their prom. Some
of the students told their teachers that they were already
celebrating. They were drinking "polaxi," a kind of wine.
Also, one student appeared at school today with $200 in
cash of his own—for the prom he said. I'm glad my son
didn't need $200 for the prom—even a new suit, corsage,
and the works didn't reach that!

May 15
       I did have ten students out of
thirty-two in my first-period class. The rest went to field
day, I guess.

During my break, I saw the white principal of Cleveland in the office. He brought back a bus-load of students. His school wasn't having field day. The students had the schools confused. Norton was *trying* to have a field day.

The Norton principal called to ask Glenview to send him help. Mr. Mulloy went, but he came back with an empty bus.

I saw Mr. Mulloy after he got back. "The students are going to field day. They might just as well let them stay. They've done this for years," he said.

I had been thinking, "Why haven't the school principals on Johnson Road collaborated and prevented this problem? Field day on the same day for every school on Johnson Road would eliminate so many problems for everyone."

Is field day worth all the headaches? Teachers and administrators have their doubts until they see all those excited youngsters.

May 17

Sunday papers are full of the integration problems. When I read about nationwide problems, I always try to relate them to the local situations. Mr. Hudson told me reflectively one day, "I had to let education go this year to concentrate on many other problems. Next year, it will be easier for everyone because we have worked out many of these problems."

I was thinking, too, about some of the problems we've at least found a way to deal with, if not completely solve. In fact, most of these problems are not going to be resolved except over a respectable time span. Being punctual for class in the morning, for instance, involves the

family patterns of the student, as well as the student himself, and these changes will come about very slowly.

"I can't wag materials back and forth every day,"
Sue said.

"Not being able to feel that materials and equipment are safe at school is an impossible situation. A handful of vandals keep the schools stripped. Something must
be done if it means having watchmen, guard rails, alarm
systems, or something else" another transferee told me.

"Negro students are going to have to learn to be
quiet in the classroom," Margaret remarked.

The schools must all be organized efficiently; without sound organization, there can be little effective teaching and learning. Reports and records must be handled
with the same degree of accuracy and efficiency as in any
other such organization in which hundreds of people are
involved.

One of the enduring goods that surely will come out
of the school crisis is that parents—*all* parents—will realize that they must become involved in the education of
their youngsters. They cannot sit on the sidelines and
watch it being done for them by underpaid teachers. It
isn't enough to make cookies to sell for the library bene-
fit, or handle the pony rides at the school fair. Parents
must be knowledgeable about what their children are
learning and how the school and home must unify their
efforts.

The P.T.A. speaker with an appealing sense of
humor could help to educate parents. The results among
the Glenview students would be progress in getting students to school with a good night's sleep, a good breakfast, and their supplies. Informing the parents of Glen-

view's expectations could work wonders if my experience with parent conferences is any indication.

White parents, in turn, will need to clear their minds of past conceptions of the Negro and watch him earn his way.

There are many problems left to work out, but this spring's experience should present plenty of guidelines to think about. Some solutions will have to be adapted. Glenview may have to notify parents by mail instead of telephone about undue absenteeism and poor school work or no homework. The general policies being made by the school board should help everyone, black and white.

This is one time I wish I were rich. I would take advantage of this television viewing. Almost every child would make "A+" on a television commercial test. Isn't it a shame education commercials couldn't be made to get messages across to parents and children about tardiness, absenteeism, and the other school problems? If I were clever enough to write the commercials, and rich enough to pay for them, I'd have a good thing going.

May 18

The students reported that they "had a ball" at the field day.

"Did you see Mr. Mulloy?"

"Oh yes, we ran into the woods until he left."

They were completely unconcerned about the commotion that they had caused Friday.

The same thing had happened at Wilson. Pitkin had field day, and all the Wilson Junior High School students had attended. It is a tradition there too, it seems.

I am immune to shock by now, but I was a little shaken when my students wanted to know what I planned to serve at the end-of-school party. I have been in the Newton school system for fifteen years and know that such a party is strictly against regulations, so I am truly confused about what this means.

At the lunch table today, we discussed this business of the students' expectation of a big party at the end of school. We could imagine the effect if all the Negro teachers did what was apparently customary and held a party lasting a good portion of the school day, and the white teachers did not. This could create more problems. It was decided to notify the office of our concerns.

A bulletin came out on the subject:

> Please inform the students that there will be no parties given at the end of school. It is against the rules of the Newton Parish School Board.
>
> If you have taken up money from any of the students, please refund it to them.

It was signed by Mr. Hudson.

So that's the end of that.

May 19

A former principal gave me a junior-high S.R.A. (Science Research Associates) set of cards to use. I took it to Glenview for this reading-hungry group. How the students have enjoyed it! Today, when we checked it, many sections were missing. Where they went, no one knows, and what anyone will do with the cards is a puzzle to me. When I mourned to one of Glenview's reading teachers about the S.R.A. kit, she said, "You were lucky if any of it is left. The insides of my S.R.A. kit were taken."

That's not all we're missing, though. Only a few of Joan's magazines and a couple of comic books were returned. This isn't too surprising, but I was surprised when we discovered ten books missing from the literature sampler. The classroom librarians had been pleased with the returns until today.

I just hope the reading materials help whoever took them.

May 20

I had a good laugh today when I saw Mrs. Arnold—five feet of dynamite—pass my room with a stick in her hand. She was quite a contrast to Mr. Mulloy, who followed closely behind her. He must be at least six feet six inches tall—the basketball player type. A little later, Mr. Hudson and Mr. Carlson came by—both with their sticks and intercoms in their hands. Mr. Hudson's voice is loud and carried over the length and width of the school grounds: "Go home! I said, Go on home!" Believe it or not, they were chasing the seniors away. After they were dismissed, when white youngsters would have knocked each other down to get away, Glenview seniors stayed around the school. They were actually having to be chased away!

I pictured Kurt at Timberlane. I don't have to ask

him to know that he was gone the second that he was dismissed. And he was thrilled silly when he learned that computer requirements forced the school board to let the seniors out two days early.

A difference shows up where I least expect it.

May 21

The new assignments were made yesterday. Mr. Hudson is going to be principal at Project 131, the controversial new school that is under construction on Leland Street just a few blocks from Glenview. Many of the Negro teachers were surprised that he took it. He should soon be ready to retire, and he could get out of this situation. If he's had problems with sixty percent white teachers and forty percent Negro teachers at Glenview, can you imagine what he'll have when the students are mixed?

I'm glad the school board decided not to mix the students here until Project 131 opens in January, 1971. Since this student-body remained all black, it gave us a chance to get the students started on the long road of adapting to more businesslike ways. Much more progress was made with the students than would have been possible in a mixed classroom. There was no embarrassment or comments about working below grade level, and the students progressed at their own rate. If these same children had been thrown into mixed classes, the range of the needs, interests, and ability would have been much greater. Then a Superman could not have done enough to provide special materials and techniques to meet all the class requirements. If this school had been mixed, it would have been a whole new ball game, and that's what I'll find when I go back.

My transfer orders also came today—I'm going back to Timberlane! I received a letter from the Newton Parish School Board informing me of my appointment as coordinator at Timberlane High School. This will be a new challenge, and I know I will owe to Glenview whatever understanding of transferees' problems I take to the job.

When I recall how I felt about leaving Timberlane, I am keenly aware of the fact that I have changed my views about the extremely unpopular transfer plan. As much as I, in righteous indignation over *my* rights, ranted and raved about the decision to send the experienced teachers, and as much as I hate to admit it now, I believe the school board made the wisest decision. How wise, only time will tell, but the small army of white teachers with years of experience behind them certainly instituted changes that will remain.

Beginning teachers just don't have enough experience to handle all the routine problems under the best conditions. The problems encountered by the transferred teachers this spring at both white and black schools were difficult enough for those with years and years of experience to draw upon. I can't imagine what I would have done if I had faced a class that didn't conform to any of those studied in "practice teaching" or "teacher training" classes. Now, once the initial job has been done in this school system, a group of teachers will not face the same situation again. The ground has at least been broken.

Returning to the "old" schools is going to require another adjustment, for the "old" schools will never again be the same.

Now I have another worry. How will I make it as a coordinator?

May 22
                    Today I told Mr. Hudson about my new assignment.

"Mr. Hudson, you asked us to let you know when we found out for sure that we are leaving. Well, I have been assigned as coordinator at Timberlane."

He started shaking his head. "Yes, I know. I really hate to see you go. If they don't treat you right, you let me know. Anywhere I go, you have a job," he said.

"Thank you. I have enjoyed teaching for you. Everyone has been exceptionally nice to me at Glenview," I replied.

Mr. Hudson said, "I'm going to talk about you. That's right! You're going to hear it. I'm going to tell people how you closed your door and did a good teaching job in the middle of all the confusion."

I didn't ask, but I wondered how he knew what I was doing. He had so many other pressing problems that he was able to visit in my room only once. We were having a history play, and the students had invited him. The noise was terrible in the halls because the senior-high students were leaving for lunch, and Mr. Hudson was surprised to see that the students had learned to "turn off" the noise while they worked.

His knowledge of my teaching failures or successes must have been computed by the formula: "no news= good news." Since I was handling my own discipline problems and not complaining, he must have assumed that we were hard at work.

May 24

This is the last Sunday to get materials together for Glenview. What an experience this has been! Now that things are working out as they are with the school board mapping out programs for improvements, I keep thinking about what Mom told me when I was worried about this transfer. "Some good will come of this," she kept saying.

Superintendent Wheat stated during the crossover meeting that the system would be better off if those who couldn't adjust would resign. Some mighty good teachers did resign, and this was not good.

But there is another side to that. For years, some mighty poor teachers have managed to hide behind the tenure laws. If rules for dismissing tenured teachers are relaxed a little under the pressures created by this situation, the system may get rid of its biggest burden—some poor black teachers and poor white teachers who otherwise would stay on forever, occupying their jobs in name only. And this will be *good*.

The new program appointing coordinating teachers to ease the problems of teachers working under the new system may salvage some potentially good teachers who need help in adjusting.

Then there is great good in the fact that programs of study will be clearly defined and thoroughly evaluated to provide a good education for *all* children.

Another good is that more responsibility is being placed on the individual student for his behavior and progress. Since the school board is formulating parish-wide rules regulating behavior, attendance, and age requirements, students, by their own failure to comply with school regulations, may lose their right to a public education. Maybe this is just the boost that was needed to get the reluctant workers and school trouble-makers to work.

White teachers won't accept excuses for not having supplies, etc., when the money has been provided. The sloppy management in that area is going to have to be done away with once and for all. Effecting the same rules in all Newton Parish schools is going to jerk the Negro student out of some old habits. He will learn to get to school on time, to be quiet in the halls and classrooms, and to practice other habits that help provide an atmosphere for learning. He will do his eating outside the classroom, and parties will be held elsewhere.

The exodus of a large group of white students to private schools is alarming, but the task of winning them back to public education may prove to have excellent long-range effects. Educators are going to be forced to present an improved program, in such a way that the people will be convinced that this American tradition—public education—is one that must be kept at all costs.

It will be interesting to see what impact these changes make on the Negro community, but this may prove the greatest good of all. "You do what you're expected to do" is the belief of a lot of people. Punctuality developed at school could have a direct carry-over to the jobs of later years. Traditionally, employers have complained about the lack of dependability of Negro workers; being tardy and absent for unexplained or unimportant reasons has been a deterrent to the Negro workman. Maybe this too will change.

Only time—and that generations away—will tell the effect of the "Big Switch."

These students and I had been together in the classroom about three months when I thought I would like to know their reactions to what had come to be called (rather light-heartedly) the "Big Switch." We had simply got to work the day I arrived and never once discussed the situation one way or another. Occasionally there were comments from the students, but there hadn't been a true evaluation. I made out a form with questions about which activities they enjoyed most and which least. The last item on the form said: "This is my reaction to the 'Big Switch' in February:"

Reactions were varied and interesting. They ranged from "I love it—that's all" to "I didn't like it at first and I don't like it now. I wish Glenview was still the same as it was at first—but I know that it can't come true." Others commented, "I lost one of my best teachers"; "I am glad some of them are gone"; "I am glad we had to switch up"; "My reaction is that I wanted the teacher I had"; "I lost one of the best teachers I ever had. At first it was not so good." Perhaps the one that fit most of the students was the wholly impartial "It didn't bother me."

May 25

The last week of school is here.

Who would have ever dreamed that I would have adjusted so well as I did? Surely not I. When I think of the sleepless nights, the nightmares, the lost weekends, the headaches, the talking, and the nausea that preceded the transfer, it all seems like a dream.

I can speak only for myself, but the "Big Switch" certainly did not turn out to be the nightmare I had imagined. Some were not as fortunate as I. Circumstances and personalities probably made the big difference.

"Your cottonpatch background was responsible," Marian commented. I'm sure that did help me to stay undisturbed about some of their expressions, such as "He meddlin' me," and their omission of parts of verbs. I had heard "meddlin'" all my life, but the Negroes on our cotton plantation said "meddlin' with me." Anyway, I knew that meddlin' meant "bothering."

That's not the whole picture, though. The administration team has been super. The Negro principal has handled the white teachers in the black school remarkably well; the Negro assistant principal has been very cooperative, and the white assistant principal has been a godsend—an efficient, tactful organizer. The secretarial staff has done everything possible to help, and their contributions were important. The other faculty members have been congenial co-workers. The eager students have been very responsive and polite. I don't mean that they are super students, but they have tried hard in the way they know. What more could I ask?

When I outlined a "catching-up" program to those who were capable, they eagerly did their best to accomplish the goals I set. I'm still shaking my head in disbelief about the progress some have made in spelling. The top group in each "block" successfully (most made "A+"; some missed one or two each day) completed the entire seventh-grade speller. That was quite an accomplishment, especially since most of the work had to be done at home. Our reading, writing, and history programs required so much time that I couldn't do any more than just call out the words for tests.

Many of the same students did quite a bit of outside reading, too, and they worked on their creative writing at home. The progress of the others wasn't as striking, but the majority worked hard to get that "good education."

We still have much left to do, and there are only three-and-a-half days left in which to work. Many of the students are concerned about not working:

"You mean we are going to do lessons every day?"

"We surely are. I believe in giving you your money's worth."

"That's not fair. We should get to play sometimes."

"We're here to work, not play, and I believe in teaching until the last bell rings. This is not something that I have just started. Ask any of my former students and you'll hear that I believe in making every minute count."

After that, they seemed to feel a little better about working up to the last minute. This was not a new policy just for them, but I could tell that I was not very popular with some of them today.

My decisions, like those of their parents, will not always be popular, but I am not running a popularity contest. I had explained that from the beginning. Instead, I hope to gain their respect by performing my job—accomplishing some educational goals. Maybe someday they will realize that the work is for their good. In the meantime, I'll bear with it.

The central office was popular with many teachers today. The assignments for next year arrived, and there were some happy faces around Glenview. The teachers had heard earlier that fifteen was the magic number for returning to their former positions, but the return-transferee plan dipped down as low as seven years of experience in some departments. Almost all the Timberlane gang will be returning.

May 26

The day started with a nightmare to end all nightmares. It was clean-out-the-lockers day at Glenview. The lockers had not been assigned according to any order. Each student paid a 25¢ rental fee to get a locker. Some had three or four; others had none. There was no way to check on the students because they had lockers in different wings of the building. The teachers stayed in the halls to keep as much order as possible under the circumstances.

The entire time that I stood there watching this bedlam, I thought about the orderly system at other schools by which each homeroom teacher sent one or two children at a time to the class's designated area. After all the students had had an opportunity to clean out the lockers, the teacher checked the whole group of lockers. The entire cleaning period didn't last more than thirty minutes. Customarily, the rest of the period was used for "free reading" or a library period or maybe make-up work. In some classes "seat work" was done until all the students had taken turns going to the lockers. But that was another world!

I didn't get to attend Glenview's graduation last night because Kurt's graduation at Timberlane took place at the same time. The teachers who did attend were pleasantly surprised. Everything was well-organized and turned out well. The only thing different was the fact that some Negro parents presented their children with checks. One was for $50, and there were several checks for less. Mrs. Arnold said that this was done at white schools years and years ago. The lunch group teased her about knowing what happened so long ago. (She's been teaching about thirty years.)

The "lunch bunch" has discussed several times the many things that Negro schools are still doing that white schools did years ago, and here's another one!

Sixth-grade graduation! Sixth-grade valedictorian! Since I've been in Newton Parish, the white schools have frowned upon anything that gave the impression that a part of a student's education was finished. To my knowledge, there has not been a white elementary or junior-high graduation since I have been here, but we learned after going to Glenview that most of the Negro elementary schools had graduation exercises.

My seventh-grade class had graduation, too, and the class was ranked, but that was back in the "dark ages"—1941—when Louisiana had eleven years of school. All the white schools in my section of the country had "grammar" school graduation then.

May 27

Central office has decided to have all schools distribute report cards the same way—mail them. This method didn't appeal to these folks, so they haven't been bringing their self-addressed envelopes. To-day, at least six brought theirs. The older brothers and sisters must be getting the message across because I don't believe these children would ever try to persuade their parents to accept this method. These seventh graders see this as causing them to lose a "fun day"—walking to school, buying refreshments, visiting with friends, etc.

These children don't view the last day the way my son did when he was that age. His school had been mailing report cards for years, and when I suggested that he might as well stop by to pick up his report card, he exclaimed, "It's just not the thing to do. Nobody goes to school the last day." How could I have been so dumb?

I notice a big difference in the view these students have about school's being almost over. It's strange—they aren't excited at all. Maybe it isn't strange, however, when you think that for most of them summer will mean more housework, garden chores, baby-sitting—and nothing but endless boredom until school starts again.

May 28

I had ridden the students so hard about the gum problem that I decided to take them bubble gum to chew on the next-to-last day. I handed it out after a brief reminder about how to chew it quietly. Immediately I realized that I had to face a problem I had never faced before. I had never heard more noise come from twenty-seven people who were just chewing gum.

I thought quickly. "The way you chew this gum today will determine what you'll get tomorrow." It worked! The mouths closed, and they chewed quietly while I showed them my European slides.

My biggest reward came about five minutes before three when my afternoon "block" class was getting things ready to leave. I said, "By the way, what have you learned since I've been here? We don't have time to list everything, but let's mention a few."

Roberta answered immediately, "New values—not to chew gum in class, to come to class on time, work in class, and read." I couldn't believe my ears. I had never used the word "values" in that context, but it was music to my ears to hear Roberta use it now.

Kurt has gone to town to get suckers for tomorrow. I'd never promise these kids something and not have it. They've told me too many times about things that they were promised and never got.

When I asked Kurt to run the errand for me, he said, "You know, in the words of my favorite Joni Mitchell song, 'You've looked at life from both sides now'!"

And I knew the words of the song well enough to say, "Yes, and 'I'm not sure I know much about life at all!'"

Live and learn! That's what I've done this year.

May 29

A day of surprises! When I walked into the office today, the students' last day—really half-a-day because school was out at 11:30—Jerry stood by the door grinning from ear to ear. "Don't stay in there long," he said. When I turned around, I saw what he had—six cold Cokes! This was the biggest and best surprise of my stay at Glenview!

"Thank you so much, Jerry," I said. Then I saw that Roberta and Joyce were with him.

"They're from the *whole* fifth-period class," he emphasized.

When I showed the office force and everyone else in sight, Mrs. Arnold commented, "That's what I call true acceptance."

No one will ever know how much I treasure this gift.

Immediately I sent the class a thank-you. Then, during the first break, many of the students came to *thank me* for *thanking them*. This wasn't the first time that I had been thanked for something that I should have done. When I took pictures of my classes, the students thanked me for taking their pictures. Even one of the teachers remarked, "Thank you for taking their pictures. That was very sweet of you." Also on numerous occasions during the semester, students thanked me for something that we did in class. "Thanks for letting us do map work," or "That was nice of you to let us give talks; thank you." I haven't been accustomed to being thanked so much.

I wasn't the only teacher surprised today. My friend, Sue, just couldn't wait to tell me that her fourth graders brought her refreshments, which they had made, and three of them got together to buy her a chiffon scarf. One gave her some fingernail polish. She was thrilled with their display of appreciation.

Another surprise greeted me when I looked out on the campus to see babies! I couldn't figure out what was going on. Later the white teachers were told that it is the custom for the Negro students to take their babies and their little brothers and sisters to school on the last day of school. Glenview wasn't the only school that had baby day, either. Peabody had it, too. I wonder if my Wilson friend's two eighth-grade girls took their babies today.

My students got a surprise today, too. The smiling faces of my homeroom students told me how happy they were to discover that we were going to "play" after all. I had assured them that I would be testing today, but I just didn't tell them how I would test. I worked out a game of historical bingo that reviewed all the history that they had studied since I came. They had so much fun.

After the game, I read them a story. This they thoroughly enjoyed. I believe they would sit spellbound for hours while someone read to them. I regret not having had the time to read *Where the Red Fern Grows,* the favorite seventh-grade book according to all seventh graders I've known for years. I believe these children would feel the same way. I would love to have watched their expressions as they followed the story of a boy and his dogs.

This wasn't really a surprise because I had learned long ago that exaggeration has been the "thing" this spring. Rumors had come thick and fast about what was going to happen to the cars belonging to white teachers ("honkies") on the last day of school. All week Mr. Hudson had felt that he needed to assure us of one fact: "All the men teachers will be on duty." And they were. So what happened to our cars? Not one thing!

May 30

The last day. Records kept me hopping all day. Even though the children weren't there, there was more than enough to do. In fact, if I hadn't had the services of a good friend, I might still be there.

When I sealed those envelopes to mail the report cards, I couldn't help thinking about the fact that the children never fully accepted the idea of missing this last day. Maybe next year mailing report cards will be old hat to them. Who knows?

When I stopped to say the usual goodbyes, Mr. Hudson was ready to talk. He couldn't have known that I had been keeping a diary every day, but it was uncanny how his words gave it a perfect ending.

"The time has come," Mr. Hudson said. "It's almost over. We've learned a lot this year." He was shaking his head as he talked. "I've studied a lot of books on school administration, but there aren't any books anywhere that taught me how to handle a predominantly white faculty—sixty-forty—with an all-Negro student body."

"Your good sense of humor and helpful, friendly way made you such a success," I said to him, and I meant every word of it.

Mr. Hudson then concluded with a poignant statement that summarized this transferee's feelings and the feelings of countless others like me: "Books can't teach it; money won't buy it. Experience is the only way to get what we've gotten this year."